Praise for The Drunkard's Path

"Thoroughly enjoyed this book! Barry offers great insights into a functional workplace and the development of one's career. I'll be quoting this in my Entrepreneurship class!"

- Bill Moylan, Visiting ant Professor
Eastern Connecticut State University

The Drunkard's Path is an inspiring and valuable book that is packed with stories, insights, and practical tips and tools for how to live a productive and fulfilling life doing what you love to do. Barry has an authentic and genuine intention to make a positive impact on the world by way of his restaurants, his leadership, and by spreading the lessons he has learned from his success in the hospitality industry. He has succeeded in one of the most challenging industries, and he has also created impactful ways to create learning, growth, and success within his teams. Barry brings his decades of insight, education, and experience as a restaurateur and entrepreneur to this book and shows us how to live, love, and create in a way that has a positive impact and brings people joy."

- Natalie Susi, University of California San Diego
Professor, and entrepreneur

"...a fascinating read that encourages newfound and veteran professionals alike to act and speak with intention. Barry draws from his own experiences to craft the perfect recipe to succeed as an employee or boss in any professional setting."

- Megan Feragne, U.S. Fulbright Scholar and
Bilingual Children's Book Author

"As Barry's business partner, who worked side by side with him in the early years when he was acquiring the wisdom he shares in this book, I can vouch for the value that is contained here! Barry has always had a way of figuring out the most effective approach to interacting with people and problems, and he has done an amazing job of compiling all of that in this easy to read and enjoyable book. This is a rich and practical resource for anyone who is an employee or who has employees, no matter what your field!"

- Eileen Day McKusick, Author of *Tuning the Human Biofield* and *Electric Body, Electric Health*

"I have enjoyed eating at Jessurun-owned restaurants since their first, The Vanilla Bean Cafe, opened in 1989. What has kept me coming back through the decades has been a certain personality that infuses them all and undergirds a culture of welcome and excellence. This book by co-owner Barry Jessurun - less a "how to" manual, more a "how come" treatise -- blends well-prepped and tested practical wisdom into a delightful philosophical broth that will have you, in equal measure, grinning, taking notes, and coming back for more."

- Brad Davis, poet & customer

The Drunkard's Path

Self-Help and Guidance for Your Career Path

From Four Decades in the Hospitality Industry

Drunkard's Path Publishing
Pomfret, Connecticut

❖ The Drunkard's Path ❖

ISBN: 978-1-7371028-0-9 (Paperback)
ISBN: 978-1-7371028-1-6 (Ebook)

Library of Congress Control Number: Pending

Front cover image by BeeTheLove/Monique Sourinho
Front cover design by Barry Jessurun
Book layout and design by Katherine Elizabeth Walsh

Printed by IngramSpark in the United States of America.

First printing edition 2021

Drunkard's Path Publishing
P O Box 285
Pomfret, CT 06258

www.thedrunkardspath.com

For My Wife & Children

The Move – a Zen Story

There was a person coming to a new village, relocating, and he was wondering if he would like it there, so he went to the Zen master and asked: do you think I will like it in this village? Are the people nice?

The master asked back: How were the people in the town where you come from? "They were nasty and greedy, they were angry and lived for cheating and stealing," said the newcomer.

Those are exactly the type of people we have in this village, said the master.

Another newcomer to the village visited the master and asked the same question, to which the master asked: How were the people in the town where you come from? "They were sweet and lived in harmony, they cared for one another and for the land, they respected each other and they were seekers of spirit," he replied.

Those are exactly the type of people we have in this village, said the master.

Editor's Note:

I was first introduced to The Vanilla Bean Café while on family trips to see my gramma. It was the landmark out my passenger window that let me know we were almost there. I could see the brown and white sign resting on a hill and be able to count the minutes before I would be able to stretch my legs from the 45-minute drive. It became the spot where we would have lunch before seeing a community theatre show. I always felt very grown-up eating there.

I have been to every restaurant in the Green Valley Hospitality Group. There are things I love about each of them. Dog Lane Café has my favorite smoothie; they put coffee in it! 85 Main's arugula salad and sushi are fantastic. Fenton River's brussels sprouts I could eat all day. The Vanilla Bean, however, feels like my second home. Barry has told me this is because it is a 'chameleon restaurant.' It was designed in a way to change based on who is in there. Sunday mornings it is a go-to for after churchgoers, and by the afternoon, the parking lot is packed with motorcycles. It turns into a musicians' lounge or an off-campus lunch spot for the local school. While this may be true, I also know it is mine.

When my grandmother developed vascular dementia, I moved my busy life, two guinea pigs, two cats, a turtle, and the resolve to leave as soon as I could from Chicago to be her live-in caretaker. 'The Bean' became the place I went to care for myself. I sat at the same table by the same window to read and breathe for a few hours. I had recurrent lunch dates with some of the regulars - a couple in their 80's who told me stories about World War II dances and studying literature at Yale. I made friends with the local artists and musicians, and as so many before me have done, I found myself falling in love with the area known as 'The Quiet Corner.'

It would have been impossible for me to have spent as much time as I have at The Vanilla Bean and not meet Barry. I believe it is impossible not to meet Barry if you are in the area long enough. We have similar personalities. Everywhere I go, I run into someone I am friendly with and am eager to catch up with them. Barry is the same.

Our business meetings are 5% business and 95% meeting about life. It is precisely how I like running a business meeting.

I was hired to edit this book the way Barry hires everyone else. I kept showing up. My grandmother has been gone for a while, but I still find myself at The Bean. We would talk a little about his book's progress, the books I had been working on, and left it at that. The day I was asked how I found clients, I said something along the lines of 'I let them find me, and it has always worked out.' I didn't know I was telling him I use the same hiring process he does.

I am part of the community Barry has created. In 2014, neither one of us had any idea what was to come. What a person sitting in a window and the business owner would create. I wasn't an editor at the time. I don't know if Barry was writing a book then.

This book, for me, is about the communities we create. I became something bigger for my community the day I chose VBC as my place to keep going back to, though it has taken years to see what was in motion. How lucky am I to be here now in this? How lucky am I to be able to see the result of the paths I have taken.

Look at all you have done, Barry. Look at the world you have created. Thank you for letting me join in the Fun. Thank you. Thank you. Thank you.

The Drunkard's Path

Self-Help and Guidance for Your Career Path

Table of Contents

The First Page

The Beginning.

A lot of people skip The First Page.

They want to move along quickly to get to the substance.

They always seem to get stuck in the middle.

Every day is a new The First Page.

Every moment of Now is a new First Page.

Do not skip The First Page.

The First Page is important.

The First Page sets the intent.

The First Page sets the direction.

The First Page sets the mood.

Anything can be your First Page.

Anytime can be your First Page.

Any catalyst can be your First Page.

A movie, a class in school, a weekend conference, a book, a friend, a stranger.

You picked this book up for a reason. You might find that reason on The First Page.

You might find it on page 42.

Perhaps you are looking for Acknowledgment, New Ideas, Change.

Everything is Change.

Everything is in a constant state of flux.

Change is easy.

Meaningful change starts with Intent.

On The First Page.

On The First Page, I tell you my intent. My intent is to empower you so you can tell your story. A story that allows you to create the person you want to be. To surround yourself with the people that also help to inspire and empower you. We all need people around us who support our story. Our story also needs to support them. This is Selfish Altruism. This book is about Selfish Altruism. I wrote this book to help you create a space in which you can take better care of yourself, so you can take better care of others who share your world space. It is to help you on your journey through this life because it is all about the journey and who we travel with, creating meaning in our lives. It is where our story of care intersects with our actions; this is what I have learned working in the hospitality industry. It is important. It is valuable.

Set your intent. Learn things. Have Fun.

Introduction

The house I grew up in had a big farm kitchen with a six-burner stove and a wall oven. We were the only people I knew with a six-burner stove. The morning sun shone through the east wall kitchen window over the sink; the setting sun shone through the sliding glass doors on the west wall and over our kitchen table. It was a big wooden table with a formica top that my grandfather had made for our family of six children that stood on the tiled floor in front of the sliding doors overlooking the pea stone terrace.

What fascinated me about that kitchen, when I took the time to notice, was the magic my mom seemed to create with relative ease in that space. When she made meals for the entire family (which was just about every day), everything was done at the same time. That was the magic. It became something that I wanted to emulate when I was older.

I remember making my first big dinner for friends; I was 17 years old, and my parents were away on vacation. I had a dinner party for seven close friends, complete with wine, tablecloth, candles, and linen napkins; I made my shopping list, did the shopping, and chopping. When I began cooking, I had to back-time the whole meal. It was great! The organization and timing that I developed by working and thinking this way has proved to be an asset for me throughout my life. I have included a chapter just on back-timing in this book. We all use this concept throughout our daily lives, but I have found that, by having a 'word' and a 'concept,' I am better able to coordinate my actions around it and be more effective in my routines.

When I was a teenager, I loved to make myself sandwiches- not just any sandwiches, works of art. My parents always had some specialty meats and cheeses around; I would use these and any leftovers I could find to create what my mom called 'Dagwoods.' At the time, I did not know what she meant; I later learned the reference to the comic strip *Blondie* that began in 1936. In that comic, Dagwood

Bumstead would make these huge sandwiches with all kinds of meats, cheeses, and other ingredients. My sandwiches were not quite as big, but they were always delicious and looked so good that I sometimes took pictures before eating them. At the time, I thought that was weird – time has proved me wrong.

Being a perfectionist about how I made my sandwiches has helped me in ways I could not even have dreamed of when I was in high school. Sixty percent of all the meals we sell at The Vanilla Bean Café, the first restaurant I opened with my family, are sandwiches. Our daily special sandwiches are often works of art and delicious, too!

Now is a good time to tell you what you may have read in the *About the Author* section. I am the President and CEO of Green Valley Hospitality, a small restaurant group in Northeastern Connecticut. When I started out with my family to open The Vanilla Bean Café in 1989, I was not planning on staying in Northeastern Connecticut. Things changed, and I have spent the intervening years working to become a better person, a better manager, and a successful restaurateur. During that time, I (with my brother and other partners) opened three more restaurants: 85 Main, Dog Lane Café, and Fenton River Grill. This book developed from my experience operating The Vanilla Bean Café and then taking that knowledge to assist with the creation and operation of other establishments. The book covers a lot about many of the standard practices we engage in daily to create a quality experience for our employees, our customers, and the community at large.

Quality and consistently good food are important aspects of any restaurant. These are only two of many areas that must be developed to have good practices for a well-run, thriving establishment. This book is about all the knowledge and practices that I have either gained or invented over my four decades in the hospitality business and the fun learning them I have had along the way. In the Appendix, you will find a section called *What Does It Take*. It covers all the primary areas or domains of knowledge that I believe a person needs to acquire, in one way or another, to operate a successful restaurant.

This book is not just about the restaurant business. It is about the practices needed to effectively run any business while also allowing you to take care of other aspects of your own life and the future you are working to create.

In this book, you will find lots to think about, new ways of seeing things, practices to engage in, and anecdotal stories. Read this book for Fun, read it for learning, and read it to help you think about how you work with other people, either as a manager or an employee. Read it with an open mind and a willingness to see something new.

"There has to be an easier way." I remember thinking those words when I was about 12 or 13 and working in my dad's office. I was doing a repetitive task, and I wanted to find a way to make it more streamlined. At the time, I could not have known that those words would be a guiding principle through my working life.

I have heard it said that laziness is the mother of invention and innovation. I am not so sure about that. I have been called many things, but lazy is not one of them. I have designed, invented, and innovated throughout my working career. I do it from an inner drive to make things better and/or easier to do (i.e., more effective).

I know that 'better' and 'easier' are subjective concepts, and I know that what I have developed as 'better' or 'easier' could not be universal in scope. Still, I have received enough recognition and support from my peers to know that what I do and have done can be called effective. I use the word effective to mean that something or action takes care of some recurrent concern, with fewer problems resulting from the solution. For example, instead of manually backing up my important data on the hard drive in my computer, I created a batch file that does it automatically daily. Here the problem is recurrently backing up data. It takes my time and ability to remember to perform the task, which I often forget. The solution was to create a batch file that ran every night without my involvement. The new problems that now occur are in the software and the network, and I learn each morning if there was an overnight problem. These new problems that require my time and attention may show up only once a month. I call that an effective solution to a problem.

Disclaimer

I am not an 'expert.' This book does not contain the 'truth.' It is not 'the best way' or the 'only way.' It is not 'right.' This book contains ideas and stories that have been culled from my experience of working with thousands of people since 1978, coupled with my own education along the way. It may appear to the reader that I believe my way to be the truth, to be right, to be the only way. However, for me, it is all flexible. If I learn or invent some new way to handle a situation that is more effective, I will work with that and let go of an old way; this is the basis of being a free thinker. Our culture is always in a state of flux. It is important to be open and ready for change as it occurs and not fight against it or ignore it. "Your beliefs do not make you a free thinker; it is the ability to change your beliefs based on new information that does." – *Unknown*

As you read, it may seem to you that I am operating a high-functioning business with employees, managers, and owners who are always very effective in their actions. This is not the truth. We have problems just like any other company or any other person. The difference here is that we work diligently to mitigate our problems, anticipate our breakdowns and find effective solutions as a standard practice. We accept there are problems, and we do not fight against them. We move with them to resolve them in a more effective and peaceful way. Like everyone and every business, we have difficult days, and we have stellar days and lots of days in between. We never reach a point where we have figured it all out. The marketplace changes too rapidly for that to happen. We rest in not knowing, and we strive for continuous learning. In between all of that, we do our best to be our best.

I do not make the claim to be inventing anything new. All you will read in this book has been done by others, said by others, written by others in various ways in a variety of different situations and settings. In this book, I work to communicate these ideas in a way that has worked for me and I believe will work for you as well. I may be able to present an idea or concept in a way that you can hear it or see it for the first time. Perhaps I frame something in a way that makes more sense to you at the moment you are reading. That is my goal when I work with my staff, and that is the goal in writing this book.

Instructions

Read this book slowly, a chapter at a time. Do not try to rush through it just to finish another book. Read in a thoughtful way; think about what I am saying. Ask yourself what you can do with the information and perspective that I offer.

Read each chapter slowly, and if the information resonates with you, read the chapter again or dog-ear it to revisit it later (and when you get to it, try reading as though it's your first time because, in a way, you are reading it again, for the first time). As you read, think of ways to incorporate the ideas into your own life and career. Have somebody else you work with and trust read the same book/chapter and discuss the ideas and what actions you could take to incorporate them into your own lives and work environments.

As you read, you will find that you may agree or disagree with what is being said. Note that, that is what you are doing but try not to focus on your assessment. Read in a mood of wonder. If you tend to be a critical reader, try considering what is being said without automatically dismissing it. We all have our own ideas and ways of being that are a result of our own histories and the cultures we live in. But just because an idea is new or alien does not make it 'wrong' or 'bad.' In many parts of the world, people eat insects. To people in the USA, this seems just wrong. If we had grown up in their culture, we would not see it that way at all. Fundamentally, it is not about being right or wrong, good or bad; it is about what is effective in the moment to change an unsatisfactory situation to a more satisfactory one – one that works best for us now and the future we are working to create. It is all relative to time and place. What works today in a situation may not work ten years from now in a similar situation. Be open to learning new ideas and be adaptable to change.

Most importantly, enjoy the book's content in a thoughtful way and make an effort to apply what works for you into your life. So, read this book with a sense of wonder. Look for your own 'truths' that might resonate with the time and place in which you find yourself.

Notice places where you may 'disagree' with me and question both your own beliefs and my way of stating things. Question, too, whatever you are learning. That is a healthy mindset. Always be open to new learning and insights. I often learn new ways of doing things from my staff. Learning opportunities are everywhere if you remain open to the possibilities.

Preface

"If you change the way you look at things, the things you look at change." - Wayne Dyer

I am not who I was yesterday. I am not who I was ten years ago. I am not who I was as a teenager. I am a work in constant progress. I am in constant change. This change happens from external sources and internal conversations. Fundamentally, it is how we all grow and learn. The more you let external sources influence and control your life, the more you are likely to feel out of control. The more time you spend on the internal conversations, the ones you have more control over, the more you can take charge of the direction of your life – and the less those external sources will exert power over you and your actions.

While this book is about what I have learned throughout my working career, this book is also about YOU. In considerable measure, this book is about Selfish Altruism and how I have lived and worked with that mindset, even before I knew the word or concept. So, this book is about helping to create a Selfish-Altruistic YOU.

When I set out to write this book, I knew it was going to be about self-care. As it came together, I found out it would be a book about Selfish Altruism, a term I first came across in a book by Richard Dawkins called *The Selfish Gene*. Dawkins says that his 'purpose' in writing *The Selfish Gene* is "to examine the biology of selfishness and altruism." He does this by supporting the claim that though "gene selfishness will usually give rise to selfishness in individual behavior…, there are special circumstances in which a gene can achieve its own selfish goals best by fostering a limited form of altruism." This I apply to us as individuals and add my claim that by taking care of ourselves in an effective way, which allows us to take care of the community at large – be it family, co-workers, or other social groups – it will allow us to create a better future, not only for ourselves but for the whole greater community.

Studies suggest that pure altruism is rare and that we will engage in acts of altruism so that they also benefit us in some way. We need to take this a step further and actively engage in selfish acts that support the community. Take care of yourself so that you are in better shape to take care of others. Love yourself so that you can then love other people.

This book is about you and the future you are working to create. As you read through these pages, you will be exposed to new ideas and new ways of thinking about yourself and how you relate to the world of work and other relationships. Reading this book has the potential to open up a brand-new space of possibilities for you and your future, but it is not just reading that will make that happen. You will have to develop new practices based on what resonates with you, and you will have to share this material with others in discussions, all the while developing yourself into a more valuable YOU. Learning anything new always takes time and mindfulness. You need to be committed and engaged with the material and develop practices to use this new knowledge to your advantage. This is true for any new learning that helps foster change.

I know of many people who read a great book and think that their life will be changed just by reading the book. We experience this, especially, when reading something that resonates with us. However, believing that we can effectively change our lives just by reading a book could not be farther from the truth. To have it make any meaningful impact on our way of living, a book's ideas and thinking need to be actively and mindfully incorporated. For change to take place, we must alter both our internal conversations and our external conversations. I recommend that, as you read, you start to practice new thinking about yourself and put into practice what you are learning while engaged with this book.

I use the word "effective" regularly throughout this book and when coaching or educating other people. I make an effort not to use words like good and bad, right and wrong. To me, these words tend to be moralistic and are "relative assessments in time." Let us look at that statement again – "relative assessments in time." What does that mean? Using the word "good," we can explore the meaning of the statement. When we assess something as good, we are only referring to the thing in its current position and in that moment or in that space/time. The same thing in a different space/time may not be good or nearly as good. There are many examples of this in everyday life. We may think having to stay home due to sickness is "bad," but because we stayed home, we were not in the carpool van infecting others. Being sick and staying home can now be thought of as being "good." So, you see, it is all very relative.

I have found that many things can be assessed as both good and bad simultaneously; this is always dependent on the observer. These types of dual assessments happen all the time at work, at home, in relationships, etc. They stem from not having full knowledge of the criteria and concerns of the situation. For example, your boss makes an assessment and a request based on her assessment, and you disagree. In many instances, both views are equally valid. You each see the situation differently based on who you are and your own concerns. I am sure you could think of numerous situations where this occurs. Dual assessments are often based on personal background and perspective.

Figure 1 - Perspective

It seems to me that good and bad or right and wrong are more about morals and less about business. These concepts could fall under business ethics, but it seems more appropriate for a business to use the words effective or ineffective. Either something takes care of a concern without betraying current and future concerns, or it does not. Current and future concerns are often specified in a business, but they may not be in all instances. For example, almost every business that I worked for did not effectively connect my work with how it maintains the business's viability and sustainability. Yet as an employee, I dealt with that concern every day, whether or not the connection was made explicit to me. As an employee yourself, you have current and future concerns. While you may be able to speak openly about some of them, it is an excellent idea to write down everything you care about and refer to it and revise it regularly. Otherwise, how will you know if your current actions are building or betraying your desired future?

I apply this conversation of effective or ineffective to the people I work with daily. There is no right or good way to make a presentation or a wrong or bad way to make one. There is only an effective or ineffective way based on the current situation. This principle allows us to design new action. Good and bad or right and wrong are dead-end conversations that do not leave room for conversation about improvement or finding a better (i.e., more effective) way.

Throughout this book, you will find that I often repeat similar and core concepts. This is not because of the trauma I suffered while working at the Department of Redundancy Department. The repetition is important because everything is interconnected. Everything relates to the core theme of this book. It is also important to recognize how we as humans learn. We do not read or do something once and then walk away somehow instantly new and improved. True, it may feel that way in the moment, but it will not be lasting. More often than not, through repetition and the accumulation of meaning, we learn and embody new knowledge. If you come across an idea or concept that you have already read about, do not assume that you have already grasped it; think instead that *'you are seeing it again, for the first time.'*

This book is written to help you change the way you look at things in your life. From there, you will notice that change will continue. With practice and with the committed help of others, life may change in the direction you desire it to go.

Happy reading! Happy learning!

The Drunkard's Path

"It's a 5-minute walk from my house to the pub. It is a 30-minute walk from the pub to my house. The difference is staggering." - Dad Jokes

"Life is a zig-zag journey, they say, not much straight and easy on the way, but the wrinkles in the map, explorers know, smooth out like magic at the end of where we go." - Ivan Doig

The Drunkard's Path is a name given to quilt patterns that have been in use in the United States since the 19th century and are a popular favorite among the more experienced quilters who love to take on a challenge. The stitch is characterized by its zig-zag pattern made of curved fabric pieces; it gets its name from the way the quilt block looks, as this pattern resembles the path a staggering drunk might take on his way home. The Drunkard's Path quilt block dates to ancient Egyptian times when this design was discovered on several Roman artifacts; it is also known as Solomon's Puzzle, Oregon Trail, Rocky Road to Kansas, and others. This block has been loosely tied to the Women's Temperance Movement in the early 1900s and the Underground Railroad during the late 1700s until the Civil War in 1862.

While this pattern can be intimidating to any beginner quilter or one who has not attempted it before, this block is achievable with a little patience and practice. Once a quilter has practiced these patterns, it opens the artist to a wider number of patterns, layout options, and possibilities.

You will find that your own life will be much like The Drunkard's Path. As you wind through the years, you will be constantly exposed to new learning opportunities. If you take on the challenging ones, you will find a wider space of possibilities will open to you.

I first learned of The Drunkard's Path in the early 1990s from Judy Bachand, a quilter and the curator of the quilt show that adorns the walls of The Vanilla Bean Café every December. When she was taking the exhibit down, I casually asked her if she had ever done any M. C. Escher-style quilting. She said that she had not, but that it might be fun. The following December, I noticed that many of the quilts were abstract in nature and design, and I said to Judy, "I thought you hadn't done any Escher-inspired quilting." She replied, "I thought you had asked me to."

For those of you who do not know M. C. Escher, he was a draftsman, book illustrator, tapestry designer, and muralist, but his primary work was as a printmaker. Aspiring to be an architect, Escher enrolled in the School for Architecture and Decorative Arts in Haarlem. While studying there from 1919 to 1922, his emphasis shifted from architecture to drawing and printmaking upon his teacher's encouragement, oddly enough, Samuel Jessurun de Mesquita. Although best known for his iconic optical illusions, his lithographs, woodcuts, engravings, and drawings express a high level of technical expertise and meticulous attention to detail. Their puzzling depictions of winding staircases and interlocking spaces offer up visual conundrums to the viewer.

I purchased a quilt from Judy's exhibit that year by the quilter D. Hervieux. In a way, I felt obligated to, but they were also terrific pieces. The one I purchased is called 'Dawn to Dusk' and is comprised of blocks of The Drunkard's Path. It resembles Escher's woodcut print titled 'Sky and Water.' At the time, I found the stitch's name rather amusing; now I find it meaningful. That quilt has been hanging in our home for close to a quarter-century. It has hung above the cribs of both of my daughters and in our family room for many years. I have included a photo of it below.

When I look back at my own life, I see a very circuitous path. When I dropped out of college, I made a commitment to myself to always find opportunities for learning from the people around me, and I have worked many places and met many 'teachers' along the way. While most of my working career has been in the hospitality industry, I have had many different jobs at many different places.

One of my friends once remarked, "How come you always seem to have the jobs the guys in the beer commercials have?" I took it as a compliment. All those jobs and experiences prepared me to be the storyteller, manager, and business owner that I have become today.

No one's career path is ever a straight line from school to career to family to retirement. We all take meandering paths along the way, some intentional, some accidental. This is how life is for most, if not all of us; with its many ups and downs, twists and turns resembling that of a Drunkard's Path. Just like learning how to quilt, you will create many more possibilities for your own life and career when you take on the challenges and the difficult projects with a sense of purpose.

The ideas and practices in this book will help you navigate your path. I like to think of it as one of the many guideposts that you will encounter along the way in your own life. When I look back, I can see my guideposts that were helpful to me—some were people, some were jobs, and yes, some were books.

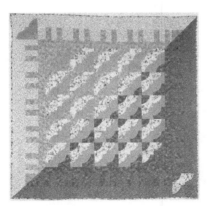

Figure 2 - Dawn & Dusk Quilt

The

Drunkard's

Path

Part 1 – Employment

"We recruit for attitude and train for skill."
- Atul Gawande

"Find out what you like doing best,
and get someone to pay you for doing it."
- Katharine Whitehorn

Important Traits for New Employees

"A new job is like a blank book, and you are the author." -
Unknown

Every day is a new beginning. More importantly, every day *offers you* a new beginning. Whether you are starting your first job or are transitioning to a new job, you get to decide the type of person you are going to be. You get to determine the type of employee you are going to be. Every new day you encounter is a space in which to practice becoming a better version of yourself. However, you cannot engage in this unless you have a plan, a story about the person you want to become in your future. More importantly, you need words that describe what you care about. These words are the traits that you include in the everyday language that you want to embody. These words have the potential to become action. That recurrent action eventually becomes what is referred to as embodied knowledge. Embodied knowledge is what we all do without thinking. We will discuss more about this in later chapters. Right now, we need to learn simple traits, or habits, that practiced overtime will shape us into the people we want to become. I have included a longer list in the Appendix, but the ones listed here are the ones that should be embodied early on in a career.

In the restaurant business, many of the traits needed to be effective at hospitality are the same traits that help us become well-rounded individuals who can function in any workplace. These simple traits should be in the first few pages of any Employee Handbook, not just in the restaurant industry. Here are the traits you need to embody every day:

Be on Time – This does not mean show up at the time you are scheduled. It means arrive ten minutes before your scheduled shift, be dressed and ready for work, clean, neat, and punched in at the scheduled time. The saying in the restaurant industry is, 'If you are

4

ten minutes early, you are on time; if you are on time, you are late.'
Be on time is listed first here because of its absolute importance. It
is the first trait by which trust is established. People who are
chronically late are often not trusted with other jobs and will not
receive promotions. When someone is chronically late, they tell
other people that their lives and problems are more important and
that their co-workers' time is not valuable. They are also telling their
managers and co-workers that they do not take seriously the
promises they make. This is not something that anyone should want
to 'tell' the people they work with or work for.

Be in a Mood of Willingness – Simply, this means saying 'yes' to
requests without causing further problems. It is also saying 'yes'
with care or passion. Every business has many situations that need
a remedy. It can be as simple as taking out the garbage to something
as complicated as preparing a menu and action plan for serving 250
guests. Employees are hired to help remedy these situations. The
primary job of an employee is saying 'yes' to requests. If you do this
in a willing manner, the whole job goes smoother and easier. When
all employees function this way, we become a Dream Team.

Be Customer-Focused –This means that you offer immediate and
quality service to the customer, any customer. This is one of the
basic tenets of hospitality. What makes them customers is that they
have a want or desire that needs to be fulfilled. If we focus on the
customer, we can easily learn the person's need and work to fulfill
it. By the way, the customer has the money, and the employee has
been hired to serve the customer so that the money changes hands
from the customer to the business. This so that the business can take
care of its financial obligations, including paying employees. If the
employees are exceptional at being customer-focused and fulfilling
customer needs, the business has the potential to grow. Learning to
be customer-focused is learning to be successful.

Be Courteous – This means to be kind and thoughtful to everyone
– customers, fellow employees, delivery people, sub-contractors,
etc. This goes a long way in creating the kind of person other people
want to be around. It is one of the traits that can lead to promotions

early on in your career. We all want to be around courteous people. No one likes a jerk.

Cultivate a Positive Attitude – This always sounds cliché, but it is crucial for success of any kind. First and foremost, you need to be at a job that you like and care about. If you are not, change to a job where you can cultivate a positive attitude. While at any job, we all want to be around happy people, mainly because the opposite sucks for everyone. Work is always easier for all when there is positive energy in the workplace.

Be Coachable – Human beings are learning machines. As people get older, they often think they have things figured out and become more difficult to coach. They shut down learning. Do not do that. Come from a place where there is always something new to learn and cultivate in yourself a willingness to learn and be coachable. Today and throughout your life.

Be Eager to Learn – This is not too different from being coachable, but it puts the emphasis on you: to learn on your own, as well as from other employees, managers, or teachers. Being in an open state of learning will open so many new possibilities that you will not know what to do with them. That is not a bad thing.

Be Willing to Do More – Employees that are willing to do more are the employees who get promoted. Show up early, stay late, take on a new task, fill in for someone. Learn a new job even though it was not requested. This trait is near and dear to me because that is how I learned so many different jobs, earned more money, and received promotions. It is what helped me to gain the knowledge I needed to own and operate a successful restaurant. From my perspective, this is one of the easiest traits on the list to embody.

Be Gracious – Be kind, be courteous, say 'Please' and 'Thank You.' Be genuine in your care for others. You cannot do anything in this world by yourself. You need people around you to help you on whatever path you are on. People like to be around gracious people. Learning to show gratitude is a skill that every person who aspires to be successful needs to develop. Beyond the workplace, practicing gratitude will help you to appreciate every moment of your life.

Be Cleanliness-Focused – This is not just for working in a restaurant. This is about working anywhere. Learning to keep your work areas clean will help you to become a more effective employee and a more effective leader in the future. Some people seem to develop this trait with relative ease, and others need to work to make it an embodied practice. This applies to all aspects of your external life, from the way you dress to the cleanliness of your car to the place you call home. It also applies to your inner life, to your thoughts and your state of mind.

Practice Acceptance – Learning to accept what is happening in front of you will put you in a more effective place when working to create change in all situations. One of the biggest problems that people have is not being accepting of current reality or situations. By not being accepting, you make the situation worse. The simple saying that applies here is: Do not become part of the problem. By not being in a place of acceptance, a person is not ready to act to fix a problem. Here is an example from the restaurant: a customer returns a meal to the kitchen. The cook can get angry and blame the server or the customer and create more of a problem, or the cook can accept that the customer was not happy and ask what needs to change to create a happy outcome for all involved. Being in a place of acceptance puts you in a position to act quickly to remedy any situation or problem.

Expect that Things Will Go Wrong – Shit happens. Really. Every day. If you enter your workday knowing that there will be breakdowns, you will be much more prepared to fix them instead of being derailed from your 'planned' day. Your plan for your day should always include being ready to fix things that will break down. Anything can go wrong, from the simple to the complex. Expect breakdowns. See the next trait.

Be Prepared – This means both being prepared for your workday and being prepared for the eventual breakdowns that will happen. In the restaurant, we must be prepared to serve a certain number of guests, but we must always be prepared to serve more or less than expected. There always needs to be a plan. Success comes to the people who are prepared for it. Preparation is a skill that can be developed into an effective trait.

Do Not Take Things Personally – Whether it is customers, fellow employees, or the boss who is speaking to you about work or the business, it is not personal. When we take things said or done to us as personal, we do not respond in an effective way. When you can focus on what you care about, you can function much more effectively instead of being reactionary to a perceived personal attack. Of all the traits listed here, this is the most difficult one to embody. We will discuss this one in more detail in a later chapter. There is also a great book called *The Four Agreements* that you should get and read at least three times. When you can embody this trait, life gets a whole lot easier.

Learning to embody these and all traits takes willingness, mindfulness, action, and time. When you begin to practice these traits, know that it will take time. You may already have some of them down. Pick one or two and focus on them until they become habit and then work on some others. Being an employee is like being paid to practice becoming a better and more effective you. If you plan on being self-employed or owning your own business, it is best to learn and make mistakes while working for someone else, or as I like to put it – at someone else's expense – before you strike out on your own. You also get to practice the embodied knowledge you will need when you are self-employed while working for another employer and getting paid to practice.

Always know that learning to embody any knowledge takes time, so exercise some forgiveness and compassion *toward yourself* as you learn and apply your knowledge. Watch out for negative thoughts that can dissuade you from your goal. Work on letting go of negative thinking; practice letting them go and cultivating new, more supportive thoughts. Instead of thinking this: "I'm just not good at this, I will never get it." Try this: "I have not been good at this in the past, but I am getting better with practice and will improve each day." We are what we tell ourselves we are. Change your words, change your story.

When I was in my twenties, I did not know about the list I have compiled above, but that did not stop me from working to embody positive traits that I thought were necessary for my success and the success of others. There are some that I did not do well with. For example, I often let my moods get in the way of being a great co-worker. If people did not meet my expectations, it often put me in a bad mood, and I would not be happy about being at work. I always got over the bad mood, but I was not only hurting myself – I was someone that others did not want to be around. I was blaming others for my bad mood. I did this for years until I was able to realize that *I* was one who was putting *me* in a bad mood and choosing to blame everyone else. Once I realized that I was only hurting myself, it became much easier to change the behavior and work toward a more effective resolution.

Beginnerhood

"You can learn new things at any time in your life if you're willing to be a beginner. If you actually learn to like being a beginner, the whole world opens up to you." - Barbara Sher

Everybody is a beginner at many things throughout their lives. Get used to it. Seek it out and do not try to get away from that feeling too fast. When we move out of the beginnerhood mindset in a new job, we often shut down possible new learning and appear incompetent to our co-workers and customers. One day at work, I had a customer call me over to complain about a rude and incompetent employee. I asked who the person was and was surprised to learn that it was an employee who was only on their third day. This employee attempted to move with certainty and knowledge because they did not like being assessed as a beginner. Instead, they were assessed as incompetent. I remedied the situation and used it as a teaching opportunity.

Being a beginner is uncomfortable, and many of us try to escape that feeling. I suggest you learn to love and enjoy it, as it is a place from which you can learn easily and grow. If you are not deliberately putting yourself in uncomfortable, 'beginner' situations, you are limiting future potential. Entrepreneur Sujan Patel, who is the co-founder of *Web Profits,* has this to say: "While it may not feel like it in the moment, a little bit of discomfort goes a long way in terms of personal development. Sure, no one likes feeling uncomfortable, but it's a big part of improving your performance, creativity, and learning in the long run."

When I work with any of our new employees, I encourage them to 'be' a beginner. Stay in the mindset and seek to be at peace while you are in this uncomfortable situation. It takes about three months to learn all that we require of a new employee, and we encourage them always to ask questions. We do not encourage the idea of 'fake it until you make it.' That is a way of being that usually causes more breakdowns and problems than necessary. We want our employees to be beginners. We want them to ask questions; we want them to be in a mental state of learning all the time.

For as long as I have been educating and training people, I have always encouraged our staff to learn as much as possible. It was not until I took a Tai Chi class in the late 1990s that I was introduced to what is called 'beginner's mind' or *Shoshin*. *Shoshin* is a word from Zen Buddhism that refers to having an attitude of openness, eagerness, and lack of preconceptions when learning a subject. Even when studying at an advanced level, it is still learning just as a beginner would. We had spent months working on a 64 form Tai Chi, or 64 movements, and had been getting pretty good when the instructor announced one day that we would be learning the forms from opposite sides. That means that instead of going left in a form, we would go right—64 different times. The instructor encouraged us to suspend what we had learned and approach the learning from *Shoshin*. The idea was to have us get back into the beginner's mind and deepen our learning. The lesson for me was to approach how I work with our employees, especially when encouraging them to learn new tasks. It changed how I worked with all new employees. I encouraged them to accept being a beginner and to stay in the mindset as long as possible. I also encouraged them to explore the idea outside of work and apply it to their life-long learning.

The ability to sit in beginnerhood, to sit comfortably in not knowing, is a superpower. Complete knowledge and certainty are fallacies and very limiting, mainly because they shut down future learning potential. I greatly enjoy working with high school and college-age people because they are malleable – in a good way. They are open to learning and do not have many hard and fast ideas that can be limiting. They are beginners and find it easier to be in beginnerhood. That means that if you are 25 years of age or older, be careful of your certainty and work to put yourself in uncomfortable situations that can expand your world view.

Now, it is your turn to practice *Shoshin*. If you are at a job, ask to learn something new. If you are changing jobs, work to be present in the moment and embrace your beginnerhood. If you can work to get comfortable with this idea and make it a life-long practice, I promise you that you will be exposed to much more learning, and your life will open up to a larger space of possibilities.

Like most people, I always tried to move away from being a beginner too fast. It was by observing that impatience in others that I was able to observe it in myself. Once I could 'see' it in myself, I was able to begin working to improve. Then I worked at cultivating a mood of wonder at everyday things. Being 'new' every day opens up a world of possibilities. However, the pull of certainty is very strong, and I am often reminded of this by my staff when I begin seeing things as certain. I am always a work in progress.

Employment is a Conditional Promise

"Do not make promises you do not intend to keep."
- Anonymous

Being an employee is a two-way street. We often do not think about employment that way and often give the employer more power than we should. When I say that employment is a conditional promise, I mean that each person in the transaction is making promises to the other, and each person has their own conditions within which they will work and be satisfied. Ideally, each party in the transaction should be more than satisfied, but there is also a minimum that each should accept before there are consequences.

The promise that an employee is making when they accept a job is to follow the rules and guidelines that are in the employee manual. In the absence of an employee manual, an employee is promising to fulfill the basic requirements of almost any job: be on time, be in a good mood, work well with others, engage with customers in a positive way, treat everyone with respect, work to help the company attract customers, and help the company be profitable. Many of these are implicit promises and often not even stated in a company manual. Some are made explicit as conditions that the company wants all their employees to adhere to while working. Many of the implicit ones are implied by the nature of the work or culture. Whether explicit or implicit or implied, it is important to try to find out all that the role requires before you fully accept a job.

You as the employee should have your own Conditions of Satisfaction while working for any company. Most likely, you have some but have never thought about them in a meaningful way. Usually, employees wait for a problem to occur before recognizing that they are not happy at work; their dissatisfaction gets them to start thinking about it. If you have a list of conditions before you begin a job, you will be better able to spot problems and breakdowns before they happen and be in a much more effective position to react to the given situation. Below are some examples of what every employee should have on a list of conditions for satisfaction in almost any workplace.

> Competitive pay for the job and area in which
> the job is performed.
> A balanced work schedule that is posted a
> minimum of 5 days ahead.
> A physically safe workplace.
> An emotionally safe workplace.
> Electronic funds transfer for payroll.
> Consistent and accurate pay each week.
> Room for advancement.
> Room to grow and learn new jobs.
> Continued education.
> No harassment or sexual harassment.

This is just a sample of what you should be looking for in an employer. This list will be different depending on the job. For example, if you join the military, a physically safe workplace will most likely not be provided. Or, if you are working at a small business, there may not be room for advancement.

Become skilled at knowing what promises you are willing to make and what promises you will not make. It is important to have these in mind when you are working at a company so that you will be able to recognize when you might be entering or already in a situation that compromises you or the employer's satisfaction.

The main thing to remember is that both the employee and the employer are on equal footing, and as an employee, you should not be settling for conditions you find unacceptable.
I often worked to change conditions that I found unacceptable; sometimes it worked out, and sometimes it did not. I left a bartending job because the manager and I disagreed on how a bar should be run. In other situations, I made requests of management

to make changes to create a happier workplace. It did not always happen. There will always be compromise; this is the way things work most of the time. Do not compromise your safety or other important Conditions of Satisfaction you may have. You always have the power to leave an unsatisfactory situation or decline an unsatisfactory opportunity.

The Golden Rules of Hospitality

"Do what you do so well that they want to see it again and bring their friends." - Walt Disney

I like to say that there are many rules in hospitality, but really, there is only one. Create a clean, friendly environment where people feel comfortable and welcome to the point that they want to return regularly. Inside of that, there are many ways that we can achieve success. The great thing about this is that it does not only apply to the hospitality industry. It applies to every workplace, relationship, living situation, and engagement that we are part of each day of our lives. Learning to be a hospitable person is a skill that you can develop, and it will significantly help with your career advancement.

Great hospitality, like any relationship, is a two-way street. A great host can only offer the highest levels of hospitality to a gracious guest. Have you heard the saying that 'the customer is always right'? Well, they are not. While we all love to have accepting and gracious guests, the reality is that not all people are like that. We all walk around wearing whatever situation our lives are in at any given moment. Sometimes it is not pleasant. Often, a customer will dump on their host the negativity in their own lives. In the restaurant business, this is acceptable up to a point. Each restaurant will have its own amount of bad behavior that it will tolerate, but it is important to recognize when to let a guest know that they are no longer welcome. This holds true in any business. This holds true with any relationship. At some point, you may have to lose a customer because they are not appreciative of what you, as host, offer and are often rude, demanding, and dismissive. You get to 'fire' them.

Perhaps you have experienced that this is also true in friendships. Sometimes you must quit hanging around with rude people and do not appreciate your genuine attempts at generous hospitality.

For most of our guests and the other relationships in our lives, learning to practice great hospitality is essential for a happy life, a satisfying career, and a good cohort of co-workers and friends.

Disney's Seven Service Guidelines:

- Make eye contact and smile.
- Greet and welcome each and every guest.
- Seek out guest contact.
- Provide immediate service recovery.
- Display appropriate body language at all times.
- Preserve the "magical" guest experience.
- Thank every guest.

Dictonary.com has this to say:

hos·pi·tal·i·ty -noun

1. the friendly reception and treatment of guests or strangers.
2. the quality or disposition of receiving and treating guests and strangers in a warm, friendly, generous way.

Develop the ability to be hospitable. By this, I do not mean just to be adequate. I mean to be warm, friendly, and generous with your time and attention whenever you can. Showing up as someone who genuinely cares for others will help you in almost any career you are in, along with creating many vital friendships. There is that saying about getting ahead in life: 'it is not what you know, it is who you know'; it is also how well they know you. If you are a hospitable person, you will be remembered, and it will go a long way toward helping to create a future that helps you take care of all your concerns. (Remember Selfish Altruism?)

Working in a restaurant you have the opportunity to meet many people. In some cases, they will be people who can be influential in your life. In some cases, you may introduce people to others who can create life-changing relationships, but in all cases, it puts you in a community of people. In communities of people we create lasting relationships that make a big difference in the lives of many.

I have met countless receptive people in the restaurant industry, mainly by being friendly and hospitable. Every day I have helped people, whether in small situations or large, life-changing ones. Sometimes it is as simple as giving directions or taking the time to listen to a parent who has dropped off their young child at the local boarding school and is struggling to cope with her new feelings. Some people stay in your life for only a brief moment, and some stay for years. As for the aforementioned parent, we became good friends and would pick up our conversation each time she delivered, visited, or retrieved her child. When her student graduated, I met family members and later shared a tearful goodbye with her.

Many relationships get their start in the restaurant industry. Restaurants are, after all, often social hubs where people go to meet other people. I know of numerous weddings that have taken place due to people meeting in one of our four restaurants. I know of many businesses that were started by people who meet each other in restaurants. I know of many of my employees who have met people at our restaurants and parlayed those relationships into rewarding jobs and careers. I should tell you that I met my wife because of my restaurant. She was a musician who was booked to play the room. As an extension of my warm, hospitable self, I asked her on a date. And her gracious and accepting response helped change both our lives.

Working in a restaurant is one thing. Embracing the hospitality nature of restaurant work is another. Simply by developing the skill of warm hospitality, you will create a different future for yourself and others, no matter where you work.

Mood of Willingness

"It's your willingness and commitment which can set everything right for you more than anything else." - Vishal Ostwa

Show up. That is the most important thing you can do in just about any aspect of your life. Show up in a mood of willingness, and it creates a much greater space of possibility for you. So, what is this mood of willingness? It is being present in the moment and being ready to do anything that is asked of you, implicitly or explicitly, while being in a good mood. Remember, the request must be in your job description, so do not just say yes to anything. There is always something to be done, either in a work environment, a home, or even in a relationship. Approach everything as if you were expecting it to happen. We will cover more on the topic of managing your expectations later in this book, but for now, you will find it easier to focus on just fostering a good mood for yourself and those around you.

We all know people who live in bad moods, as though it is their job. We all have experienced a situation where one person with a bad mood can sour everyone's mood. The opposite of this is also true. One person, radiating a good mood and willing to work at whatever it takes to get a job done, will positively affect the whole group. Be that person: at work, at home, in your relationships.

We all have and experience moods. I often ask people, 'Do you have moods, or do your moods have you?' In other words, are you acting a certain way at a particular moment based on a mood that has nothing to do with that moment? When we act this way, we can cause further problems and breakdowns for ourselves and others. Acting out of inappropriate moods can be a career killer, a relationship killer, and in other cases, can create an environment where others do not want to be around you. There is a section on moods later in the book that will cover more on this topic. For now, we will focus on working at cultivating a mood of willingness in small situations, like helping at home or working with a specific group of people at work. This is a skill to develop, but you build trust with others and integrity in your life with this skill. Trust and integrity are important traits to have when building a career, while building a life.

Early in my career, I was often plagued with bad moods that I blamed on the people or the situation around me. Someone once said to a group of people, of which I was a part, "Barry is not happy unless he is in a bad mood." That was the catalyst that I needed to begin looking at my response to my everyday situations, and I began taking responsibility for my moods. First I worked on not blaming others for my moods, and then I worked at developing my overall mood and the mood of the workplace. Even after doing this for years, I would often fall into the trap of a bad mood that had a negative effect on all my co-workers. Now, as the leader of an organization, it is important that I manage my mood and work to create the mood of the environment, a space where my staff can also work and be in a good mood.

Working with Others

"Individual commitment to a group effort--that is what makes a team work, a company work, a society work, a civilization work." - *Vince Lombardi*

The real title of this chapter should be 'Relationships.' Another title I considered was 'Plays Well With Others.' No matter what you do in life, you must coordinate with others to produce a result. It might be with co-workers in the same office or colleagues in a different state or country. It might be a vendor or customers. It is all about coordinated action to produce a favorable outcome. Throughout every day, in all that you do, you will be working with others (unless you are a hermit, in which case you would not be reading this book). You will be beginning, building, and solidifying relationships. It is important to know that this work of coordination with others is the main action you will be engaged in throughout your life. Practice it, get good at it. Make it an embodied practice. I must repeat this because it is so important. Every project you engage with, every product or service you consume, every good relationship is produced by coordinated action. It is all about working relationships – with co-workers, vendors, colleagues, and customers. This is also referred to as teamwork, but in this chapter, we will focus more on the conditions that must exist to create a team that can work effectively. It is all about creating functional relationships.

We all experience difficult people with whom we must work. Where you have the power, short of waving a magic wand to change them, make the changes necessary to remove or marginalize these difficult people. If you do not have the power to make this type of change, make requests to the people who have the power to do so. If they are unwilling to make the necessary changes, always do your best to work with difficult people. Be clear in your requests, commitments, timelines, and promises. Follow up effectively and communicate clearly.

Throughout my working career, I have always worked to create an environment that contained people with whom I wanted to work and be around. It was not always possible. I would often make requests of managers to step in and fix or mitigate a problem with co-workers. Sometimes they were unwilling or unable to do so for reasons that I was not aware of in the moment. In these situations, I took it upon myself to be the better worker and do my best to surround myself with better workers. Often, I would ask not to be scheduled with a person who got through each shift by always doing the least possible amount of work. When a schedule solution was not possible, I had to work on my mood and my level of work and not let anyone else affect my work ethic or attitude.

When I was in my twenties, I worked part-time as a lift attendant at a ski area. I worked three days a week so I could get free skiing and make a little extra money. I was bartending as a regular job and enjoyed skiing on my days off. At that time, in that area, the kind of people who worked in the lift department were not your high-rising top performers. Often, they had good summer jobs and just needed something to do in the winter or people who were unemployed and needed any job. Many of them did not even ski. After I had been there about a month, I figured out with whom I wanted to work and on which lift. So, I requested to work with them on that lift. The boss was reluctant to do so, mainly because the people I requested were the best employees, and he did not want them all together in one spot. He finally agreed, and we created a great team that worked well, both together and with the customer. From a safety and hospitality standpoint, we were so good at our jobs that we received mail addressed to our lift, and customers would bring us gifts. The point of this story is that you have the power of observation, and you can make requests to help create a better work environment for yourself and others. Again, this is Selfish Altruism at work, and it is an important way to help create and foster change.

When working with others, you must make an effort to foster well-functioning relationships and create the environment within which you want to work with the people you want to work with. Always do your best and do not let another's attitude or lack of a work ethic affect how you do your work.

I have witnessed many disagreements and battles at work. While the disagreements were in the open, either with the management or among a group of peers, the battles were usually subversive. I have observed that many individuals are not effective in voicing their displeasure, and most do not know how to wage a 'subversive' battle in an open, effective manner.

First, let us examine disagreements and voicing displeasure. If you can see that a supervisor's request is doomed to be ineffectively fulfilled, there are many courses of action, all dependent on the situation as a whole. There are a few important actions to keep in mind. Do not engage in a disagreement at the moment of the request – unless you assess it as an unsafe situation. Always take time to make a full assessment of the requested task. When voicing your disagreement, always have a solution ready-at-hand. Do not voice a disagreement without offering an alternative solution. By failing to offer a solution, you become a part of the overall problem.

Subversive battles occur all the time. They are very subtle, but their long-term consequences can be very damaging to all involved. Fortunately, there are ways to look at a problem and engage the battle in a manner that has a better outcome for everyone. For example, in the Café, when I have two prep cooks, there is almost always a battle that occurs. It happens like this: prep cook A does all the work necessary for the day, but the day's end is busier than expected, so cook A leaves some work undone. When prep cook B comes to work the next day, he/she makes the assessment that cook A has deliberately left that work for them to complete. If this happens enough (usually just a few times is all it takes), prep cook B will start to leave work for prep cook A deliberately. When prep cook A chooses to make the same assessment of B and begins *deliberately* to leave extra work for the next day, the battle is joined.

The problem is that they have engaged in the wrong battle. In this battle, everyone suffers. Other employees now must pick up their slack; we run out of product more often, so the customer suffers. This affects consistency of our overall offer, so the whole restaurant suffers.

In the above scenario, the battle has been to see who can do the least amount and leave more for the other person. Let us declare the battle in a different way. We must first ask ourselves what this is about. I declare that it is about integrity and value, and because of that, it is also about money since people get paid based on their integrity and workplace value. So, if it is about money, how should we engage in a subversive battle? If cook B makes the assessment that prep cook A is leaving extra work, then B should do the extra work and a little more, so that at shift's end, no work is left for cook A. This way, cook B gets the hours and the kudos, while prep cook A is left with fewer hours – and so, less pay. In this case, prep cook B makes more money and will be valued more by the employer and employees alike because extra work does not fall to anyone else, and the customer does not suffer; overall, the restaurant runs smoothly with a consistent product. This scenario is still a subversive battle, but the consequences are focused. Prep cook B makes more money, is valued more, and so comes out the winner.

Of course, the prep cook's job is to prep the food necessary for the restaurant to run smoothly with fresh, quality products. It stands to reason that there is always work to do in the prep kitchen. When these battles show up, they are a false creation in the minds of the individuals involved. There really is no battle. It is all just problems that they invent and engage in to squeeze more meaning into their lives. I have noticed this to be the case in most employee disagreements and subversive battles.

As an employee, it is important to notice these battles and work to create a harmonious work environment. This takes time, commitment, creativity, and energy. But it is almost always worth the investment. In the long run, it is the manager's job to help create these environments, but help from the employees always goes a long way.

The 'Yes' Path

"If somebody offers you an amazing opportunity, but you are not sure you can do it, say yes – then learn how to do it later!"
- Richard Branson

When I was thinking about this book, I had initially thought this chapter should be called 'Keeping Promises.' A promise is one of the five main Speech Acts that we all engage in when we utter or say anything. Making and keeping promises is a skill that is vital in any relationship. We will cover more on Speech Acts in the Management section of this book. Here we will cover what it is that an employee does simply by accepting a job. They promise to say "Yes" to requests (and in our restaurants, we require that the 'yes' be in a mood of willingness). The 'Yes' Path can be seen in Figure 1 below.

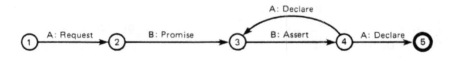

Figure 3 – The 'Yes' Path

This path is part of a larger diagram called 'A Basic Conversation for Action' that we will cover more thoroughly in the Management section of this book.

As an employee, you promise to say "yes" to requests. It is that simple. You need to become an expert in being a promisor, someone who makes a promise. That is where the 'yes' comes in. An employer or manager makes a request, and an employee says "yes" to that request. That is how things get done. That is how businesses get started, how buildings get built, how offers get fulfilled, how countries get started. Someone makes a request, and someone else fulfills that request. That is the simplest form of an action workflow that keeps everything going.

What is interesting about the world of work (and life in general) is that we all make Promises and Requests every day. What we do not often think about is that they are *conditional* promises. There are certain conditions under which I will say "yes" to a request. As an employer, we are bound by the laws that govern our country, state, and industry, as well as our own story of our business, which shapes the requests that we can make. As an employee, you are also bound by many of these same things, but you will also have your own conditions inside of which you will be a willing promisor. For example, an employee of a certain religious faith may have a condition that they cannot work on Sundays, or a single dad may say that he can only work during school hours. These are the conditions under which they will say "yes" to a request. The list of conditions can be long or short. The list can be governed by many other factors in our daily life: family responsibilities, the weather, or the geographic location of the business.

As a young person in the workforce, I became an excellent promisor. I almost always said "yes" to explicit requests, uttered by the boss, or part of the job description. I also became good at taking care of and fulfilling implicit requests. Implicit requests are the requests that are 'implied' by the work environment. The requests do not have to be made out loud or explicitly. For example, in the restaurant industry, there is always something that needs to be cleaned. So, it is always right, because you can see that it needs to be done. Just step up and, without having to be asked by a boss or manager, clean something that has been overlooked or take something apart for a thorough cleaning.

This saying "yes" to requests, both implicit and explicit, is a skill I developed early on in my working life. I would step up and do the job, sometimes the most difficult job or the one that other people ignored. In our restaurants, it is this type of employee that we look for and then work to educate and train for advancement. We will sometimes leave things undone just to see who steps up to do the work.

The caveat to this 'Yes' Path is that the requests must be in line with your job description and be ethical as well as moral. For example, I can request that an employee wash my car. They get to say 'no' because it is not in their job description. However, I can ask them to wash my truck if we are going to be using it for catering. In that case, it is part of their job description, and they can comply with my request. Employers will often take advantage of an employee by making requests that are outside of their duties. It may start off as something simple but could progress to jobs that fall completely outside of the job description. Many employers will abuse their position of power over an employee, so it is best to learn how to say 'no' to requests that are not appropriate. As always, there is plenty of gray area here, so use your discretion wisely with any and every employer.

Becoming a good promisor will help to open other opportunities in your career. Continually fulfilling on requests in a mood of willingness will set you apart from many others in the workforce.

Richard Branson, English business magnate, investor, author, philanthropist, and founder of the Virgin Group, which today controls more than 400 companies in various fields, knows a lot about saying yes. The quote at the beginning of this chapter says a lot when you take a look at what Mr. Branson has achieved during his business career, just by saying 'yes.'

Teamwork

"There is no such thing as a self-made man. You will reach your goals only with the help of others." - George Shinn

So much has been written about Teamwork that it seems almost comical. The fact is that everything we engage in involves Teamwork. Most of the time, it is conscious Teamwork, where you can identify all members of the team and what their specific jobs are relative to the task at hand. Teams can be in the same room, or across the globe, or anywhere in between. Literally, everything is accomplished by Teamwork in one form or another. Even using toilet paper in a bathroom requires so many people it is almost impossible to account for them all. From lumber harvest to paper mills, from transportation and warehousing, all the way to your bathroom, there are hundreds of people who made that roll possible.

With Teamwork, it all comes down to coordinated action for the sake of producing the desired outcome. The more you realize that this is how virtually everything gets accomplished, the more you will recognize the value of Teamwork and, more importantly, being a valuable member of a team.

Teamwork in the restaurant industry is one of the most visible forms of Teamwork that can be witnessed regularly. It all happens in the same building in short bursts (i.e., breakfast, lunch, and dinner) and in longer time horizons (i.e., workday, workweek). It also involves sub-teams working together to create a smoothly functioning larger team. For example, there is the kitchen team that creates and cooks the food, the service team that serves and cleans up after a meal, and there is the management team that coordinates and oversees the entire process. All these teams must function as independent teams while also being aware of and working as part of the larger, overall team. This coordinated dance is a joy to watch when it functions smoothly, but it can be like witnessing a train wreck when it does not function well. One of the most extensive breakdowns I have witnessed is when the independent teams do not realize (make real) that they are part of the whole. Oh, they may get it right on a written test, but they do not yet embody the knowledge. When an employee embodies knowledge, it means they can, having gained both big picture and task-specific understanding, accomplish the required tasks without thinking about what they are doing; they just do. Their smaller actions always have them show up as someone who is thinking about the larger picture, the other teams, and the desired outcome. Which, in most cases, is customer satisfaction.

In my experience, it takes strong leadership with a greater sense of purpose to create the story of effective Teamwork. A leader focuses on the individual players and mobilizes them to be dedicated to the larger picture by not just taking care of their jobs in the moment but also by realizing how their contributions affect the whole team and the desired outcome. Strong leaders attract dedicated team members by creating a space in which effective Teamwork is the automatic outcome. These leaders create the possibility of effective Teamwork. The team fulfills on this possibility, and when done consistently, it creates stunning results. We all have been on stellar teams and always look forward to even more meaningful work like that.

The importance of Teamwork in your life is everywhere. It shows up at school, at home, at work, and even at play. The more you recognize that you are always a team member and that others are relying on you to accomplish what you have agreed to accomplish, the more you will begin to value yourself and your contribution. The more you increase this value in yourself, the more you are motivated and mobilized to take better care in the moment so that you can create a more effective outcome in the future. It essentially helps you to embody a stronger work ethic because you know you cannot do anything alone, and you need people in all aspects of your life to help you succeed. You are also part of someone else's success. Accepting and embodying that you are a great team player will help you achieve your own life's goals.

The more I realized that my contributions to a team were necessary for everyone's success, the better I became for myself and my team. I worked more thoughtfully. I worked longer hours and took on new challenges if necessary. I was rewarded with promotions and raises throughout my time working for other businesses that I did not have to ask for. It was because of my knowledge of Teamwork and how it is vital for any organization that I was able to excel.

At The Vanilla Bean Café, the kitchen and service areas are small and positioned right next to each other. Everyone on the team sees everyone else on the team and can communicate effectively with each other most of the time. Kitchens are notoriously noisy places to work. With equipment running and the hood fans making even more noise, it can be hard to hear at times, but we can see each other, and that is what makes the teams there function exceptionally well.

I have worked in other restaurants where the workspaces are separate and sometimes on different floors. In that environment, it is much more challenging to function as a cohesive team. In these types of restaurants, the team is segregated into smaller teams with specific tasks. In these places, the team will be further separated through language as well as physical space; terms like Front-of-the-House or Back-of-the-House are standard. It can be further broken down to specific jobs like bartenders, servers, cooks, dishwashers, etc. I have noticed that when these smaller teams are not included as part of the whole, overall service suffers. Many servers will act like independent contractors, running their own service business inside the restaurant. Bartenders may do that as well. It takes strong leadership to bring these smaller teams together to make them feel that they are part of a whole organization aiming to create that five-star dream team. It is much harder to create the dream team in full-service restaurants.

In a limited-service restaurant like The Vanilla Bean Café, where the team is working together in a small space, this is much easier to create. When I designed Dog Lane Café, I approached the design from this idea of Teamwork that is supported by the layout of the physical space. All the team members can see each other almost all the time due to the open kitchen design. I even took this idea a step further and designed it so that all the employees could see most of the customers – as a reminder about why we are here and who the customers actually are. Creating a team that functions well relies not only on the design of our physical space but also on the 'design' of our overall story. And so, every day, we are all reminded why we are here and who we work for and with.

The next time you see one of those cliché Teamwork posters at work, give it some more thought and the respect it deserves. More importantly, think of ways you can improve yourself through deepening your understanding of Teamwork and then work to become a top team player.

Who Do You Work For?

"This is the real secret of life -- to be completely engaged with what you are doing in the here and now. And instead of calling it work, realize it is play." - Alan Watts

When I was in my late teens, I found that I had trouble with the concept of working for someone, not the actual working part itself but the notion that I worked for someone else. I started to think that I was working for myself because, after all, who was I doing anything for anyway? Myself and the future that I was working to produce.

I never stopped working for other people; I just positioned myself in the forefront as the one for whom I worked. I found this to be incredibly empowering. I was motivated to do things for myself. I found that if I did what I thought was my best in a consistent manner, it was easy to outperform the competition. I was promoted faster, I received pay increases sooner, and I got to make my own work schedules. I did this all for me, but everyone benefited.

In those early jobs, I encountered people who labored under the idea that they were working for someone else and never rose to their full potential. I heard it from their mouths. They would often say that when they were working for themselves, they would put more into whatever they were doing, but they certainly were not going to do it for _____(insert name here). This seemed lazy, just a way to avoid doing more or extra work. I also saw it as a way of shutting down possible learning, learning that was available at someone else's expense, learning that would help them toward their best possible future.

I watched many people practicing mediocrity in their work habits and attitudes with the idea that they would do better when they were doing exactly what they wanted to do. To me, it seemed that they were practicing being a mediocre worker. If and when they ever got to, "do what they wanted to do," they would be so good at being mediocre, I am not sure they could rise above it. What they practiced, they would become.

There are great learning experiences in all aspects of work, but many people choose not to experience them for various reasons, like "I'm not being paid enough," or "This is not what I plan to be doing in the future," or "It's not in my job description." Excuses to shut down learning abound.

I always looked at specific tasks as learning opportunities and did not care if they were not "in my job description." It did not matter because I was working for myself, and I wanted to learn everything I could…, at someone else's expense. Let me offer an example of a learning experience I encountered. When I was working at a ski area in the lift department, we were charged with preparing for the addition of a new lift for the next season. Our job was to mark out the path through the woods so that the trees could be cut down to create space for the lift construction. The problem was that the engineers had not marked out the centerline. We had to begin our job, but the engineers had not done theirs. They would not be back for several weeks. It looked as if the job was going to be delayed. Not one to be deterred, I suggested that we use the transit and the target that had been established and shoot and mark the centerline ourselves. With some reluctance on my partner's part, we set out with tape and transit and got to work. To complicate the mood a little more, it was cold and raining. Long story short: when the engineers came to do their job, they found that over the 1,400' of forest that we covered for the lift, we were only 1 inch off the centerline that they established. We had Fun and learned a lot. More importantly, because I did this for myself, everyone in the project benefited — except maybe the engineers.

Often, I encounter people who see this idea of working for oneself as simply being selfish and therefore "bad" or ineffective. There is a paradox in this way of being. Chinese Philosopher Lao Tzu in the Tao Te Ching states that, "True self-interest teaches selflessness."

A tad esoteric, I know, but it is a way of being in the world that is astonishingly effective.

What appears to be selfish on my part – my "working for myself" attitude – actually takes care of the whole and all involved, manifesting as selflessness. This is because I never forget who makes it possible and all the co-workers, without whom I could not do anything. This may sound like I contradict myself, but I also work for them. I have found that if I identify the best outcome within the given structure of the business or task at hand and I work (for myself) to achieve that outcome to the best of my abilities, everyone wins. This is *Selfish Altruism*.

I have been the direct manager of well over 1,500 people during my work experience. There have been only about 5% of all those people that I would want to work with again. The top 5% all have an attitude and work ethic that is selfish but works out to be selfless. "Always do your best," seems like a cliché, but it is what makes the top 5% of all the people I have managed shine. They know that they work for themselves. Because they work for themselves, their work environment is a better place for all.

I have developed a way to teach this way of thinking and working. All the new hires in my business receive this training. It is based on an action workflow circle, but it is really about an employee's work environment. The basic model of this is below.

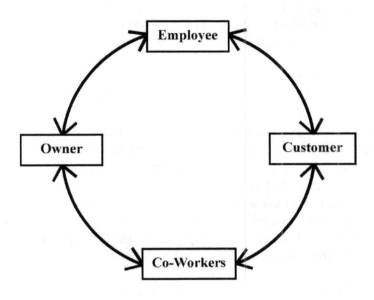

Figure 4 – Who Do You Work For?

This workflow circle's basic idea is that there is no one specific starting place, hence the arrows pointing in all directions. Because it is designed for the individual employee, they are at the 12 o'clock position, and I use that as a starting position when explaining it to people. I will take you around this circle with the conversational strategy I use.

So, 12 o'clock: As the owner, my first question to an employee is, "Who do you work for?" Their commonsense answer is to point at me and say what is obviously true to them, "You." Or they may say the name of the business. So, I ask the question another way, "Who told you to apply for a job here?" The answers at this point are mixed. My final question is, "Who do you have to satisfy each and every day of your life?" At this point in the questioning, they all get that it is themselves they are to satisfy, whatever they choose to do.

Here are two other related questions I like to ask: "So, who are you doing this for?" or "Are you here because you have some story of the future that you want to get to, and by working here, will help to get you one step closer to that future?" I conclude this phase of the conversation with one final thought, "Work here because YOU want to work here – for YOU!"

Ok, onto 3 o'clock on the workflow circle. *"Now* Who Do You Work For?", at this point, some people tentatively point at me, but some come up with the answer – 'the customer' – all on their own. Basically, the customers have the money, and I am in business to provide what they want in exchange for what I want (their money). So, I hired you to help me get it from them. In exchange for that service, I promise to pay you for your help. You see, I cannot do this alone. I created a business here that promises a product and service to many customers each day, and I need help to fulfill that promise. By hiring you, I solicit a promise from you to help me fulfill my promise to the customer.

It is not just about that one customer; it is about all their family and friends. I want their money, too, so that I can grow my business. Therefore, you must take care of the customer beyond their expectations so that they tell their family and friends to come and try our product and service. I might lose a sale because an employee has a bad attitude toward a customer. The employee may say that it was only one sale – "What's the big deal?" What the employee does not realize (until I tell them) is that one lost sale could amount to many more lost sales in the future. Sears (a large retailer) tells their salespeople that a Sears customer represents $250,000.00 to Sears over a specified time. If they screw up a microwave sale, they potentially screw up a quarter-million dollars worth of sales in the future. The bottom line here is to always take care of all customers beyond their expectations.

6 o'clock: "Now Who Do You Work For?" I often get, "It's not you, is it?" No, it is not me. Can you do this by yourself? I cannot; that is why I hired you. Your co-workers are your customers, too; you need to satisfy them. They show up every day expecting you to show up and be a great member of the team – and they need to satisfy you. I am sure that you have your own Conditions of Satisfaction for the kind of people you would like to work with. So does everyone else.

You need each other. Your job as a new employee is to show them that they also need you. Show up as someone who cares about what *they* are doing and who they are doing it for. Showing up for others is deeply valuable and will have long-lasting effects on your future.

The owner makes this all possible, understanding of course, that many other forces, too numerous to go into here, also contribute.
9 o'clock: The owner. In our cultural common-sense way, you work for the owner. But remember, if you are satisfied with your work, and the customer is satisfied with your high level of service, and your co-workers love you, then the owner will be automatically satisfied.

Note the arrows that point from the owner to both the employee and the co-workers. It is a smart owner who never forgets that they also work for their employees. As an owner, it is my responsibility to create and maintain a work environment where both employees and customers want to return. The details are numerous but include a fair wage paid in a consistent manner (no bounced checks), a clean workplace, an effective schedule of work, properly maintained equipment, possibilities for advancement, etc.

I believe that this apparently selfish way works because it teaches the employees to mobilize themselves and emphasizes that there are others in the equation who need to be satisfied. This is a basic form of leadership, and teaching it to the people who work for you – and with you – produces effective results.

We have been practicing this owner-employee conversation at The Vanilla Bean Café for a long time. I find that when an idea becomes part of the culture, the employees will make fun of the concept and play with it while at the same time embracing it. One busy day I was checking in on the prep cook who I knew was up to his eyeballs with a lot of other stuff. I asked him how he was doing, and he replied, "My boss is an asshole." I immediately asked him who he worked for. He quickly responded with a thumb to his chest and said, "Me!" I said, "That's great! Sorry to hear that about your boss." That round went to me.

So, Who Do You Work For? Who do your boss and co-workers work for? And if you are the boss, who do your employees work for? And oddly enough, who do each of your customers work for? After all, if they did not make the effort to be your customer – ideally an easy, low-cost customer – we would not even be talking. The point here is that if all our customers were difficult, self-centered, and concerned about no one else (i.e., failed to function well in the workflow circle above), they would be high-cost customers. High-cost customers reduce profit margins and generally produce a bad mood, neither of which is good for long-term business potential and growth.

Work for yourself and the future self that you are creating in a selfish, altruistic way. Always do your best, show others how, and demand it from all your customers (i.e., co-workers, customers, vendors, other business owners). This produces results in the present moment and more effective results in your future – all the while, it makes life a little easier.

Don't Take Things Personally

"Nothing other people do is because of you. It is because of themselves. All people live in their own dream, in their own mind; they are in a completely different world from the one we live in. When we take something personally, we make the assumption that they know what is in our world, and we try to impose our world on their world. Even when a situation seems so personal, even if others insult you directly, it has nothing to do with you. What they say, what they do, and the opinions they give are according to the agreements that they have in their own minds." - Don Miguel Ruiz

When I first began working in the restaurant industry, we called the process of learning how to work with people in such a close environment and with the hundreds of customers every week 'de-sensitivity training.' If you were a sensitive person, overly aware of the people around you, easily affected by their actions AND unprepared to handle those actions effectively, working in this type of environment could be difficult. With commitment, time, education, and training, you can learn to be appropriately 'desensitized' to the people and the unbalanced energy around you.

After many years of working with people, both co-workers and customers, and continuing my own education, I have learned to look at this a different way and speak of it with different language that more effectively takes care of myself and others. To make it easier to teach and discuss 'de-sensitivity training' with others, I like to refer to it as not taking things personally.

In a stressful work environment, like a busy restaurant, it is easy to take a comment from a co-worker in a personal way. Reacting to this situation in the moment just causes further problems. Almost nothing anyone can say to you is personal. If I call you a 'jerk,' whose problem is it? Your automatic reaction is to think it is your problem and one you must respond to in the moment. The problem resides in me making an inaccurate assessment of you based entirely on my own thinking and history. In a way, it has nothing to do with you. I might call many people 'jerks' for various reasons in various situations which is all about me, not you. You get to say, "Thanks for your assessment. Have a nice day.".

When a customer is being rude, it is not about you. They are just rude. For reasons of their own, they may blame you, but you do not have to accept the blame. You can think, "too bad you are a rude jerk," and still carry on with your job. Do not make other people's problems your problems. It is so easy to take things personally, and we give into it because it seems so real. But the reality is that people walk around being who they are independent of you. You just might be a trigger in their environment that causes them to act. It is not your fault; you do not have to take it personally.

Suppose you think of it as someone giving you a gift you do not want. Perhaps it is a book that is of no interest to you or one you have already read. If you politely decline and do not take it, it is still theirs. The same is true of anything else they give you, be it anger, rudeness, or anything else you do not want or need. You get to let them keep it.

I work with many young people, and there is not a week that goes by that I do not have to help an employee navigate this topic, be it about a co-worker or a customer. I have had had employees in tears due to the mistreatment of a customer. The employee takes this burden on and takes what the customer said, not realizing that it is the customer at fault and that they do not have to take on their problems as their own. This is easy to say but very difficult to practice. I coach my staff regularly about this topic, and I see many of them begin to improve and become more effective in taking care of themselves in these situations.

Learning this skill is vital in the hospitality industry, but it is also valuable in almost any work environment. There will always be difficult managers and customers. Learning the practice of self-care through not taking things personally will help you immensely in every relationship you have and advance your career.

There is a great book that you need to read that goes into this on a much deeper level. This book is called *The Four Agreements* by Don Miguel Ruiz. To deepen your understanding of the quotation at the beginning of this chapter, it would be best if you purchased the book in audio format and listened to it a minimum of three times. Share the book with others and engage in discussions to deepen your understanding and to begin the work of embodying this knowledge. Embodied knowledge is knowledge that lives in your body and your actions, without the need for thought to activate the action. It is developed with practice. Think of any athlete in any sport. If they are a professional, what they get paid for is embodied knowledge, not for their understanding of the sport or how well they can do on a written test. They get paid for actions that they know how to do because of their practice. In order to learn a new skill, it is important to practice that skill. Practicing with others deepens and broadens that skill.

Not taking things personally: this is a skill to develop. You just do not read about it once and think, 'wow, that is great, I will do that.' Embodying new knowledge does not work that way. I meet so many people who have read a book like *The Four Agreements* and call it a life-changing book. It certainly feels that way when you read it. Three weeks after they finish the book, they cannot recall any of The Four Agreements. If something you read is meaningful, you need to read it again. You need to discuss what you have learned with others who are like-minded. You need to practice.

Learning not to take things personally is like learning a martial art. First, you hear about it and think it is a good idea. Then you get a teacher and start learning the history and philosophy of the art. Then you practice moving your body and then begin learning with others in the somatic dance. With time and practice, you become proficient, but it takes time and practice. In the beginning, you get knocked on your ass a lot. As you progress in your practice, you find that you do not get knocked down quite so much; you are able to keep your somatic center, your body's center, in a more stable way. You still get knocked down, but you recover much more quickly. Your reaction time becomes quicker, and you often move without thinking. Think of your body's center as a place of balance from which you have a maximum capacity to act, a place where you are at ease yet ready to move in any direction. If you were to watch two martial masters in a discourse, like Aikido, you would see them move quickly, reacting to their opponent with skill and ease. It would appear as though they never lose center. However, it is just that when they lose it, they recover their center so quickly that it is not noticeable.

What the martial arts masters do with their bodies, they also have to do with their minds. Their minds must be focused and immersed in the story of their martial art. I refer to this center in the mind as the linguistic center. The linguistic center is made up of the stories we tell ourselves about our past, present, and future. When you work to find your linguistic center, you need to create stories about yourself, your past, your present, and, more importantly, your future. You need to know what you are working to create. When you have a vibrant story about the care you need to take in your future, the actions you need to engage in to help manifest that future, you can more effectively act in the present moment. When you engage in actions that are not in step with your future story, you have lost your center and are no longer in a space of maximum capacity to act. This can create situations that are damaging, not only in the present moment but also for the future you are working to create.

Creating this linguistic center is the starting point for not taking anything personally. The other aspect of not taking things personally is found in the quotation at the beginning of this chapter, "Nothing other people do is because of you." What other people do is based on their own stories and often because of a lack of a coherent and effective story on their parts. They are almost like the ball in a pinball machine, bouncing and 'flipping' from place to place, believing that they do not have any options at all. All aspects of their life are 'happening' to them. It is the false belief that they do not have options. These false beliefs are a part of their linguistic narrative, and this creates the reality they help to generate. Throughout their lives, they have made decisions that generate a reality that leads them to act and speak the way they do. It is not you. It is not even about you. You are a trigger in their environment, that is all. Their actions and words have nothing to do with you, so you do not need to take their actions and words personally. What I recommend is to watch "the show" with detached bemusement, learn what you can, take the action that the situation requires so you can take care of your own future, and move on.

If what someone says to you causes you to feel personally attacked, you need to look inside of yourself to find out why you feel this way. It has something to do with your past and the stories you tell yourself. While the scope of this book does not include help in this area of psychology, there are many ways to examine your reactions to other people's words and actions. My favorite is the Buddhist way of examining your emotion and going fully into it and accepting it. It is through this practice that you can find a way to come to peace with the emotion and its roots so that you can fully accept it and what it has to teach you. You should not be reactionary to the present moment due to unresolved problems in your past. Being nonreactive takes work, and I believe you can do the work necessary to achieve this.

There are many practices you can engage in while working toward not taking things personally. I found the following from www.elephantjournal.com by Lindsay Carricarte:

When you find yourself sinking into offense or experiencing hurt feelings, use these seven tips to stop taking things so personally:
- Ask yourself if this is true. What is true in this situation?

- Consider for a moment if what is occurring has anything to do with you at all. If it does, own your part of it. Or are you just the person who ended up being there at the wrong time? Put the feelings aside for a moment and think rationally and analytically.

- Ask yourself why you are hurt. Why are you allowing the situation to hurt you?

- Pause. Do not jump to conclusions. What you are assuming you know is more than likely clouded by emotion.

- If you find yourself stewing over what happened, bring your focus to something else. Read a positive book, go help someone who needs it, hang out with some animals (especially dogs), or do something to focus your attention elsewhere. Take your mind off the event until a later time.

- If needed, give yourself space. Go for a walk or work out, connect with nature or the water element, do a yoga flow, or call someone and see how they are doing. These tasks boost self-esteem and confidence, which will bring the perceived problem into a more realistic perspective.

- Repeat this mantra: "Not my circus, not my monkeys. That is all about you, not me." It usually hurts because we care what people think—which is a setup.

The Tao Te Ching offers this: "Care about people's approval, and you will be their prisoner."

The truth of the matter is this: Once we care about what others think of us and we chase after their approval and validation, we take everything they say and do personally. We become their prisoner and slave.
I say, "F*ck that!" Do not allow another person to put you in that position.

We can remind ourselves that what people think or say about us is none of our business. Their negativity has little or nothing to do with us, but rather everything to do with who they are and where they are.

Learning to not take anything personally is a very freeing skill to learn, and it makes you invaluable in relationships and in the workplace. You will find that your career moves forward much quicker when you act from your own linguistic center, your own stories, and do not react to the stories of those around you. You want to be the star in your own story, not a minor part in someone else's story.

Below you will find some ideas on how to stop taking things personally:

Stop Worrying About What Other People Think

It does not matter what people think of you. What does matter is what you think of yourself and what people you know, love and care about you think of you, and that is it. Strangers and acquaintances offering their opinion of you has absolutely nothing to do with you. What they have to say is always about them. So, stop caring what other people think and focus on your own sense of who you are.

Maintain Your Self-Confidence

When you know and appreciate who you are, you will not have time for what other people think and say about you. Having self-confidence and knowing your self-worth is the foundation on which everything else is built: your achievements, your relationships, your ability to keep going when life and work get tough. Doing the work to create a strong sense of your worth will show in every aspect of your life, personally and professionally.

Do not Jump to Conclusions

Based on scientific studies, it has been noted that when people make an assessment about you or offer critiques, they are rarely about you. "In fact, it's almost always about them, their issues, their needs, and their desire to control you and/or a situation," writes Dr. Abigail Brenner. To help manage your response to difficult situations, it is good to know what your own triggers are and be prepared when they are about to be pressed and respond in a prepared and measured way.

Let Things Go

Look at painful experiences as lessons, and practice how to better navigate bad situations. Do not let them make you angry or bring you down in any way. Use them to create a better and stronger you, and then move on. When you do not let things go, it does more damage to you than to the other person. See the appendix section called AFFIRM for more on this.

Fill Your Calendar with Things you Care About

It is hard to find time to think about other people and what other people think if you are busy. Fill your life with family, friends, and work that brings you joy, and prioritize accordingly. Chances are that you will not have time for other people's negative assessments.

Do Not Sink to Someone Else's Level

When someone is disrespectful or cruel to you, the worst way to respond is to reply with more negativity and toxicity. Do sink to their level and become a part of the problem. It may feel good in the moment, but the long-term consequences will likely be something you regret. Take the high road and move on.

Ajust Your Attitude

"Our lives are not determined by what happens to us but by how we react to what happens, not by what life brings to us, but by the attitude we bring to life. A positive attitude causes a chain reaction of positive thoughts, events, and outcomes. It is a catalyst, a spark that creates extraordinary results." - *Anonymous*

Early on in my career, I did not know about this skill called 'attitude.' When I first learned of the concept, I was able to create meaningful practices around it and become a more effective person. I must admit that there were times when my attitude sucked, and I was not an effective employee.

At one job, they had an employee of the month declaration, and I did not like how it was run or (sometimes) who was chosen for the honor. Because of my bad attitude about the practice, I worked to subvert the competition by putting the company cat on the ballot and asking everyone I knew to vote for the cat. Oddly enough, the cat won. What management did was both surprising and instructional. They acknowledged that the cat had won. After a thorough investigation, they found that the cat did not have any of the proper paperwork in the human resources department, so they awarded the honor to the person with the second-most votes. Their humor and grace helped me to observe my own attitude and adjust it for the remainder of my employment. With work and practice, I was able to overcome my bad mood and moved toward being an effective person and team member.

When we use the word *attitude*, our cultural way of thinking has us relate it to a person's way of thinking and being. We think of it as a psychological construct, a mental and emotional way of being in each situation. This could refer to a positive or negative way of being. Another way of thinking about attitude is to see it as a cool, cocky, defiant, or arrogant way of being – that is generally unacceptable in a work environment.

The attitude that I am championing here is a positive one that helps to generate more positive actions and moods in the environment. An attitude is a predisposition or a tendency to respond positively or negatively toward a certain idea, object, person, or situation. Attitude influences an individual's choice of action, as well as their responses to challenges, incentives, and rewards.

Four major components of attitude are:

1. Affective: emotions or feelings.
2. Cognitive: belief or opinions held consciously.
3. Conative: inclination for action.
4. Evaluative: positive or negative response to stimuli.

When working with co-workers and customers, all the aspects of attitude come into play. Your attitude defines who you are and will influence how you see the world around you. It will also help to shape your future. The work environment is what it is; the attitude brought to it by all the workers is what shapes the reality of the environment on any given day. The attitude of the owners or managers will shape the space of possibilities within the workplace. What does all this mean, and what can you do about it?

It puts all the power in your hands. It is quite simply the power of choice: the choice of where you work, the choice of what environment you want to be in, and most importantly, the choice of your own attitude in any given circumstance.

In our culture, we tend to cast blame on everyone and everything but ourselves. I have been in places where everyone seems to be given a 'blame thrower' when they arrive. This attitude is counterproductive to the self and to the group at large (and to the rest of the world, but that is for another book). When we blame others, we give up our power. We surrender to what we think is "out there." Working to create your own attitude, regardless of environment and circumstance, will empower you and help you produce a better and more effective workplace and future.

Viktor Frankl was a Holocaust survivor and the author of *Man's Search For Meaning*. He made this observation, "We who lived in concentration camps can remember the men who walked through the huts comforting others, giving away their last piece of bread. They may have been few in number, but they offer sufficient proof that everything can be taken from a man but one thing: the last of the human freedoms - to choose one's attitude in any given set of circumstances, to choose one's own way." Are you choosing your own way, or are you letting others choose it for you?

When I worked for a ski area in New Hampshire in my early 20s, I looked at all the jobs available on the mountain. I decided that being a lift attendant would offer me all that I was looking for at the time: good hours, free skiing on my off days, and the chance to meet almost everyone who was skiing on each day. I was there to have fun. I found out that most of the other lift attendants were not there to have fun. They needed a job; this was a job. Most of them did not even ski. They certainly were not there to have fun. I managed to find the one return employee from the previous year, and together we worked to change the environment.

At that time, the lift maintenance department head was also in charge of all the employees. It was not an aspect of the job he enjoyed, to say the least. Very little attention and training were given to the employees, and the mornings were shaped by a dark mood in the shop where we had to check-in. The makeup of the environment was shaped in part by this manager, who did not foster a fun environment for the employees. I am not sure he even thought about it. I could see why there was only one return employee from the year before.

I did not let the atmosphere of the department get in the way of my goal of having fun at work, and we did have fun. The lift I worked on the most would sometimes get mail from happy customers. My sense of fun permeated the rest of our crew, and the customers had fun as well.

At the end of my second season there, I put in a proposal to the new head of the department. I proposed creating a new position in the department, a position that was focused on the hiring, training, and education of lift personal. The position was also in charge of creating a positive daily environment for all the employees. By the end of my fourth year there, the lift department had a better than 50% return rate for employees, and we had reduced the number of lift-related incidents for both the customers and the employees. The lift department also earned the rank of third in safety for mid-sized ski areas... in the nation!

In hindsight, I can see that it was my attitude that helped to foster change in the workplace, most importantly for myself but also for the employees, my co-workers, and the customers. Other departments also benefited from our department's changes, especially in their ability to work with a positive attitude.

I approach each day with a positive attitude. I work to help foster a positive mood in the kitchen and on the floor. Some days it is easier than others, but I make it a priority every day on the job.

Have you ever come to work and found that the place seemed to be in a bad mood? You might even have walked into an establishment as a customer and felt the same thing. Something is wrong; the energy is off. Most often, this comes from the leadership, who are generating it themselves through inadequate and ineffective practices (or just being jerks) and allowing bad moods and attitudes to be prevalent. Strong leadership takes responsibility, first and foremost, for their own moods and attitude and then works with employees to function with good moods, not allowing bad attitudes to permeate the workplace. Managers and employees who indulge in their bad moods and attitudes are selfish jerks. If you work for one, find a way out. If you are one, find a way to change. While it may feel good to indulge in a bad mood or attitude, a feeling you may even believe that you are entitled to have and broadcast, it is not productive and is very damaging to your career in the long run.

There is a book called *The No Asshole Rule*. This review from Booklist sums it up quite well and reinforces my point about managing our moods and our attitude:

"We all know them or know of them – the jerks and bullies at work who demean, criticize, and sap the energy of others, usually their underlings. It could be the notorious bad boss or the jealous co-worker, but everyone agrees that they make life miserable for their victims and create a hostile and emotionally stifling environment.... [No asshole] rules have transformed such companies as JetBlue, the Men's Wearhouse, and Google into shining examples of workplaces where positive self-esteem creates a more productive, motivated, and satisfied workforce."

This transformation starts by learning how to manage our own moods and attitudes first. Then you can learn how to help others. The teacher Jesus put it this way: "First remove the log out of your own eye; then you can see clearly to remove the speck out of your [co-worker]'s eye." If you are in a position of power, by learning to manage your own moods and attitudes, you will gain the clarity and wisdom for helping – or releasing – an employee who may be good at their job but disastrous for the team.

Changing your attitude does not happen overnight – it takes practice and, most importantly, a willingness to change.
The following has been in our Employee Handbook for so long I do not know where I found it. It is there for fun and learning, but to also show how important Attitude is to create the life you want to have.

1. It is your attitude at the beginning of a task more than anything else that will determine your success or failure.

2. It is your attitude toward life that will determine life's attitude toward you. Despite many people's belief to the contrary, life plays no favorites.

3. You control your attitude. If you are negative, it is because you have decided to be negative and not because of other circumstances.

4. Act as if you have a good attitude. Remember, actions trigger feelings just as feelings trigger actions.

5. Before you can achieve the kind of results you want, you must first become that person. You must think, walk, act, and conduct yourself in all of your affairs as would that person you wish to become.

6. Treat everybody as the most important person in the world.

7. Attitudes are based on assumptions. In order to change attitudes, one must first change one's assumptions.

8. Develop the attitude that there are more reasons why you should succeed than reasons why you should fail.

9. When you are faced with a problem, adopt the attitude that you can and will solve it.

10. We become what we think about. Control your thoughts and you will control your life.

11. Radiate the attitude of confidence and well-being, as one who knows where you are going. You will then find things happening to you right away.

12. In order to develop a good attitude, take charge first thing in the morning. Do you say, "Good morning, Lord" or "Good Lord, morning"?

"Don't mix bad words with your bad mood. You'll have many opportunities to change a mood, but you'll never get the opportunity to replace the words you spoke." – Unknown

Relativity – Good/Bad – Right/Wrong

"Good and bad, right and wrong, are relative assessments in time."
- Barry Jessurun

"There is nothing either good or bad, but thinking makes it so." -
William Shakespeare, Hamlet

Good and bad, right and wrong – these are words and concepts that do not belong in the effective management of a business and often complicate a very simple situation; this does not mean that a business cannot be good or bad, or right or wrong morally. Read the papers or listen to the news to find out that people, and the businesses they are involved in, can engage in immoral actions. My claim is that these words are not necessary in the management of a business, whether speaking of its owners, managers, employees, or customers.

A business makes an offer of a product or service; they market this offer and hire people to fulfill on this offer. There is a way to work in and for this business that helps to take care of all the business's concerns, including but not limited to customer service, employee relations, and business finance. The 'way' is often specified in the mission statement and employee handbooks. It is not the *right way*. It may not even be the best way, but for the sake of consistency, it is the effective way. Assuming the mission and handbook are carefully written, anything that does not fit the 'way' of the business will be ineffective, not wrong or bad.

When managing employees or in any conversations you may have, work to avoid using these words. Replace them with the words 'effective' or 'ineffective.' An action is effective if it takes care of one or more of the business's concerns. An action is ineffective if it does not take care of the business's concerns and/or causes negative breakdowns and betrays the business's concerns (i.e., loss of customers, loss of money, negative press, etc.).

By the way, using these words is not good or bad, or right or wrong. It is just that they can be ineffective in achieving what you are working to achieve.

So, how does this fit in at our place of work? When we train employees, we do not use these words. We encourage all the supervisors and managers to let employees know if an action was effective or ineffective. Does the action or situation take care of the business, its customers, and employees, or does it cause some form of breakdown that is counter to the operation of the business?

I once had a barista who had worked at another coffee shop tell me that we were making cappuccinos the wrong way and then proceeded to tell me how to make a cappuccino. At that time, I had been making coffee drinks for well over fifteen years and had training from an Italian company in Rhode Island on proper coffee extraction and beverage making. While I admitted that we were not making a 'traditional' cappuccino, we were making a consistent one that helped to sell more cappuccinos based on how it 'looked.' I acknowledged that their assessment was correct from a traditional point of view. Our way of making them was also correct based on how we chose to make and serve cappuccinos for the past fifteen years. I told the employee that when she opened her own coffee shop, she could make cappuccinos any way she wanted to make them, but while she was with us, she would make them our way. Not because it was the 'right' way but because it was 'our' way. Starbucks has created a multinational company by making coffee drinks the 'wrong' way from a traditional point of view. It did not matter to that company's growth or success. They are so good at this marketing that, in our café, when customers order a macchiato coffee, we must ask them whether they want a 'Starbucks macchiato' or a 'traditional macchiato.' Most want the Starbucks Macchiato, but many are happy with the traditional one as well.

Managers are taught to review their actions when taking care of a situation. It goes something like this: a manager makes the assessment that a situation is unsatisfactory (or ineffective). It is stressed that they do not use the words good or bad, right or wrong, in their assessment. The manager engages in action to change the situation to a satisfactory one. The manager then makes a new assessment of the new situation. Is the situation better or worse – was the action effective or ineffective? If the action were ineffective, what could have been done differently? We ask them to reflect on their actions and think about other possible actions that could have produced a more effective outcome. There is a saying that people learn from their mistakes. In my experience, that is not true. People can only learn from *reflection* on their mistakes, along with a *willingness to improve* in the future. That stance is crucial for learning to make long-lasting changes.

By the time most people start their first job, they have been inundated with these four words: good, bad, right, wrong. These words have a long and varied history that carries with it some emotional baggage, even sometimes pain. When we tell someone in a work environment that what they did was 'bad,' an emotional barrier is triggered, making it very difficult to manage the employee in the 'present moment' because an emotional response from their past has been triggered. I know of many managers who report about not 'getting through' to an employee. They cannot get through because the manager had used 'bad' or 'wrong' in the situation, and the employee put up a barrier (almost always on a subconscious level).

This choice to not use these four words in business management could also build positively toward more effective families, schools, legislatures, etc. A little honest reflection on your own history and past reactions to negative assessments will likely reveal that when you reacted poorly to those assessments, it was because you felt judged moralistically as 'wrong' or 'bad.'

By keeping moralistic language out of management situations, we can be more effective in our overall management practices. We can be more effective in training and educating our employees. Learning how to speak with people in a way that does not trigger an emotional reaction will go a long way in creating effective teams in your workplace.

I will often tell the following story to people to help them better understand this idea:

Who Knows What's Good or Bad – a Taoist Parable

An old Chinese farmer lost his best stallion one day and his neighbor came around to express his regrets, but the farmer just said, "Who knows what is good and what is bad." The next day the stallion returned bringing with him three wild mares. The neighbor rushed back to celebrate with the farmer, but the old farmer simply said, "Who knows what is good and what is bad." The following day, the farmer's son fell from one of the wild mares while trying to break her in and broke his arm and injured his leg. The neighbor came by to check on the son and give his condolences, but the old farmer just said, "Who knows what is good and what is bad." The next day the army came to the farm to conscript the farmer's son for the war but found him invalid and left him with his father. The neighbor thought to himself, 'Who knows what is good and what is bad?'

The Blame Game

"Blaming is pointing out there, rather than in here, into your own mind, when you find yourself in a painful or uncomfortable experience. Blame means shifting the responsibility for where you are onto someone or something else, rather than accepting responsibility for your role in the experience."
- Iyanla Vanzant

I have constantly been exposed to what is call the 'blame game' in my work experience. This is when a co-worker or leader blames a negative situation or outcome on the actions of others. For ourselves and in leadership, blaming others does nothing to fix the problem at hand. It deflects or shifts the attention away from the person who has the most power to fix the problem. In my studies, I have heard this type of behavior called *blame-shifting*, which is when someone moves the burden of the problem to others who are involved, and in some cases, to people who were not involved at all. We often see this in politics.

We have all seen this type of behavior through our lives, from the playground to our own families. If you have held a job at all, you see it in your co-workers and in management. If you watch TV or read the news, it is also rampant in our society. In the workplace, blame-shifting accomplishes nothing toward fixing a problem. What I am saying here is that blaming others is a very ineffective way of taking care of ourselves and the people around us. To learn how to stop blaming others, we need to understand ourselves and our reactions to what life and work throw at us each day. Self-care and learning how to be reflective and committed to improvement are crucial for resisting blaming others in the situations we find ourselves in each day.

Self-care is the most important thing for all of us to engage in on a regular basis. This includes examining how we treat others in stressful situations. Blame happens when the person blaming is focused on looking at a situation as if from outside of it and seeing themselves separate from the situation. This outlook absolves them from any blame. It does not help to fix the situation. In most cases, it will make the situation worse and create other ineffective situations in the future. People will learn not to trust a person who is constantly blaming others.

Dr. LaSharnda Beckwith, from the book *It is Your Life; Own It!: No Blame, No Excuses,* has this important bit of advice:

"Whether we like it or not, our lives are a compilation of our experiences. If we have viewed all that has happened in our lives as being out of our control, therein lies our first problem. If we blame others for any or everything that has happened to us and take no responsibility at all, therein lies our second problem. . . .The first step in turning your life around, in changing your attitude and in becoming the person you really want to be, is to first become aware of whom you have become."

Managers and leaders who are effective in their roles have learned to take responsibility in every situation. By taking responsibility, they can engage in effective action to rectify the situation and make it a learning experience for all those involved.

There are many crucial components in the restaurant business that must function together to create a successful work environment, and hence a successful restaurant. We all work together to get things done. One of these areas is weekly inventory and ordering. The main idea is not to have too much perishable inventory or run out of important items. I have worked with many managers who excel at this weekly task, and I have worked with many who never seem to get better. Can you guess one of the main actions that set these two apart? The person who constantly blames others when we are out of important items or ingredients never sets themselves up for improvement because they are blaming others for something that is their responsibility. If these people took the responsibility completely, they would be able to make changes and develop practices that mitigate the problem. They never get to do that because they shift the blame to others for their failings and insist that it is the other person who needs to improve. While we rely on all our staff to communicate their needs or see something running low, we know that this does not always happen. Good managers know this. It does not absolve the manager from doing their work effectively. Doing weekly inventory and ordering is a practice. As with any practice, the more you engage in it and with it, the better you become. If part of that practice is blaming others for your failures, there will not be any improvement.

We work with our managers and staff to take responsibility for problems and not shift the blame to others. It is always a more effective way to handle any situation and create a more favorable outcome. It is where learning takes place. They also become much better at their jobs and more respected by their peers and others.

Something else I find strange is that when someone breaks something, they would rather hide it or leave it for someone else to find than to let management know of the problem. I find that employees will also accept that something is not working or broken and not let anyone know there is a problem. This acceptance of working with something that is not working properly or broken happens all the time. My guess is that they do not want to be blamed for the problem and would rather work around the issue than be a part of getting the broken thing replaced or fixed. This is all very counterproductive behavior. Most managers want their employees to work in the most effective way that they can. Tools have been put in place to make a job easier. I am sure that they would want to know if something is not working. I know I always want to know if something is not working properly. When I visit our restaurants, I will often ask, "So, what needs fixing?" There is usually something. I suggest you get into the practice of letting management know of anything that is not working properly, especially if it directly affects your ability to do your job in an effective manner. It does not matter whose fault it is; it just needs to work properly.

I always found it more effective to take responsibility for a negative situation and alert the higher-ups to the problem. Shifting the blame and/or avoiding the blame causes further problems. When I worked at the ski area, I would often contact ski patrol or customer service when a customer encountered a problem with our staff or the machinery that might result in an injury or complaint. This readied those departments to deal with the problem and often mitigated further problems. For example, if a skier was hit hard with the lift as they loaded and it may have caused an injury, I would call ski patrol and have them meet that chair number to check in with the skier. As well, if customer service is aware of a problem before the customer shows up to complain, they are in a better situation to deal with the problem in an effective manner and create a satisfied customer. It always disarms an unhappy customer when the management is already aware of the problem before the customer even reports it. Mountain management appreciated that I did this and taught all the staff to also engage in this type of reporting. The overall result was that it both helped employees handle problems and worked to create more effective resolutions for customers without shifting the blame to anyone.

The caveat here is that owning up to a mistake is hard to do in today's culture. In my experience, many people would rather hide a mistake and hope it is never found out, or shift the blame to another, than step up and admit responsibility. Teaching people to own their mistakes and take responsibility is a difficult task and an uphill battle in our culture. I have been teaching this for over 35 years and still have difficulty getting my point across.

Taking responsibility is a leadership move. It can also open a place of deeper learning. This quote from Vishwas Chavan, the author of the best-selling book *Vishwa Sutras: Universal Principles for Living*, sums it up quite nicely, "Admitting a mistake is not a weakness; on the contrary, it shows an openness of your heart. It takes guts to say sorry. Only a strong and well-balanced individual with clarity of mind can do so effortlessly. Taking responsibility for your actions requires and develops your self-control. You become your own person." I will also add that it is powerful.

In essence, when you admit your mistakes and accept the blame, you become a problem solver, not a problem maker. When others see that trait in you, they will want to be on your team, and other future possibilities will open for you.

Common Sense/Acquired Sense

"If you want your employees to deliver excellent service, you'd better provide them with excellent leadership." - Lee Cockerell

A common mistake people make is thinking that there is this thing called 'common sense' that everyone picks up simply by being awake. This mistake causes more breakdowns in everyday interactions than most people realize. There really is no such thing as 'common sense' in the usual sense of the phrase. We use the term to indicate a baseline for what we expect everyone we work with to know, and then we communicate with people assuming they have this baseline of knowledge. Problem: it does not work (have you noticed?), and this stems from our own belief that there is this thing called 'common sense' that everyone has.

While I have bumped into this mistake throughout my working career, there was one event in particular that helped me realize that I had to create the 'common sense' for our restaurant. A new employee had answered the phone and did not have the answer for the customer calling. I asked the employee to put the call on 'hold.' That employee did not have a clue as to what I was asking. It was at that time that I took the education of the staff much more seriously and started to put many of our practices and policies into writing. I could see at that point in time that it was up to me to create this common sense and not to rely on something that did not exist in the way I thought it existed. I really thought that any person living in the United States at that time knew what a 'hold' button was.

You know what it is like; you ask someone to do something, and they say they will get it done. When you check on the outcome of the work, you find that something is very wrong. Although I do not think that anyone really needs one, I will give an example, but that would be me thinking that all readers have a 'common sense' about this – and I could be incorrect in my assumption. In the restaurant business, we use refrigeration a lot to keep perishables from perishing. You may think that it would be common sense that refrigerated items need to be kept under refrigeration. So, the request goes something like this: "Please empty and clean that refrigerator and then restock it neatly." When we check on the progress of the job, we find all the perishables out on a table in the hot kitchen. What are you thinking – do not you have any common sense? These things need to stay cold. The problem is not that the person does not have any common sense. The problem is in the request; the person making the request thought that there was this thing called common sense. The request should have been phrased more like this: "Please empty that refrigerator and place all items in the walk-in cooler. When that is done, thoroughly clean this refrigerator and then restock it neatly with what you had placed in the cooler." Of course, that directive still leaves room for ambiguity; what exactly is 'neatly'?

Everybody in a specific environment has what I call 'acquired sense.' Acquired sense is the knowledge that a person has gained throughout their lifetime. It will be different for each person for a vast number of reasons. There are certain kinds of knowledge that may be common to a certain family, or a certain neighborhood or city. There will be some common knowledge among those from the same cities or countries, but there is no 'one' common sense. The restaurant industry is known for its fun and playful jargon, and learning whatever jargon is used in any job is vitally important. It is part of the 'acquired sense.' One of my favorites is 'In the Weeds,' which refers to both the front and back of house staff and it is used to describe a situation where the staff is pressed for time and required to work extremely quickly in a stressful environment. I was often In the Weeds on weekend nights behind the bar at a busy nightclub where I worked.

So, seeing the problem, what can we do about it? We can use to our advantage the fact that people *acquire* a common sense based on their life encounters. It is up to you as a manager to build and revise the common sense for your business. You educate and train employees constantly to have the common sense necessary to work in your environment. As an employee, it is up to you to gain the common sense of the workplace. If there is no education system and training for this, perhaps you can help invent one.

In a sense, what every workplace should be doing is inventing a new 'reality' and language base for all their employees and customers. Along with perfecting the product and service that is being offered, this act of invention takes work and consistency in the overall development of a highly effective workplace. This 'reality' becomes the common sense of the workplace, and when it is created and in place, it will then be much easier to make requests and have them fulfilled. If you rely on a mythical 'common sense' to help you, you will always find that it does not exist the way you think that it exists. So, in a sense, you create your own problem by not taking an active part in the creation of and the learning the 'acquired sense' for yourself.

"If You Say So..." How We Shut Down Possibilities
(and Create New Ones)

"If we understood the power of our thoughts, we would guard them more closely. If we understood the awesome power of our words, we would prefer silence to almost anything negative. In our thoughts and words, we create our own weaknesses and our own strengths. Our limitations and joys begin in our hearts. We can always replace negative with positive." - Betty Eadie

"We are often our own worst enemies." You have most likely said this yourself or have heard other people say it. I believe this to be true. Earlier in this book, you learned about how the words we use help to generate our realities. This is also true when it comes to our own 'self-talk.' Our internal conversations have a way of manifesting in our outward realities. Your words have power.

Your own internal conversation, your self-talk both limits and expands your possibilities. By constantly repeating and believing your own inner conversation, you create your outward reality. If you say something like: "I have always tended to talk too much," it is your truth. You make it so. However, it is not *'The'* truth. You tend to talk too much because you give yourself permission with your own thoughts, not because you talk too much – it just seems that way. You can begin to change your way of being simply by changing your internal dialogue: "I used to talk too much, but I have been becoming a better listener lately."

Contrary to negative self-talk, positive self-talk will have positive effects on your outward reality. If you say something like: "I am becoming a really good listener," then, if you are not just flapping your gums, you will become more aware of what the other person is trying to communicate.

This may seem all esoteric and weird, but I have seen this in action countless times, and perhaps you have witnessed it as well. You may have even engaged in such inner conversation throughout your life without realizing what you were doing. I can look back on my younger years when I changed my internal conversation to change my outer reality without knowing what I was doing. I simply saw that something new was called for, so I launched the new inner conversation. I saw that what I had been telling myself was, in fact, limiting my prospects for growth and success. A new quality of self-talk seemed necessary and achievable. My decision to take control of my internal conversation and make the necessary conversational shift was entirely reasonable and not a bit 'new-agey.'

The simple fact is that you have this ability. You have the ability to witness your own inner thoughts, and you have the power to begin the process of changing an unproductive or ineffective internal conversation. When you realize that you are self-limiting yourself, you can be more motivated to do something about making the change necessary to change your life.

Our restaurants are what we say they are. Through our marketing and advertising, we engage in storytelling. The better we are at telling our story, the more it will take shape in the marketplace. The better we are as storytellers to our staff, the more effective the restaurant will be in fulfilling its offer to our customers and the community at large. I was not good at this early in the business. I thought that employees and customers could just 'see' what we created, that the employees could just act in a way that fulfilled my story without any effort on my part. This caused a lot of breakdowns with many different stories about our restaurant circulating in the marketplace. While I cannot completely stop that from happening, I can mitigate it by being better engaged in storytelling. Repeatedly.

I found that without clear and consistent guidance, employees would make stuff up in the moment. This caused consistency problems with our product and overall offer. Once I noticed that there were many conflicting stories about us out there in the marketplace, it took us years to regain control of the story told our way. The fix came in several forms: an Employee Handbook, a recipe book, consistent messaging in marketing, an in-house quarterly newsletter, use of social media, plus many other smaller, practical ways to tell the story.

Once we became good at saying what we were, we actually became what we were saying. This dynamic proved true for us as individuals and for our business. I believe that this is also true for humans in general. Sadly, the opposite is also true. If we are good at telling a negative story about ourselves, then we develop the capacity to create an unflattering life.

The stories we tell ourselves, about ourselves, help to shape our reality and future. If you say so – so it is. Be careful with your words. Be mindful with your story. It is your belief about yourself that creates your story and hence your reality. In the words of Henry Ford, founder of Ford Motor Company: *"Whether you believe you can or not, you're right."*

Working with Difficult People/Customers

"The greatest stress you go through when dealing with a difficult person is not fueled by the words or actions of this person – it is fueled by your mind that gives their words and actions importance."
- Mark Chernoff

"Why are some people so rude?" There are countless reasons why people are rude during interactions with their fellow human beings. The main point to remember here is that whatever is happening, it is their problem. They could have just received a speeding ticket, or maybe their son/daughter is in trouble, or their favorite pet just got crushed by a cement truck. Why they are rude is not important. They just are what they are in the given moment when you encounter them as a customer. Your job is to offer gracious hospitality.

Our automatic reaction is to think that they are being rude to us because of us. That is not the case. They are just being what they are being; it is we who make the assessment that they are rude and are being that way toward us. Now, the assessment of rudeness is most likely correct, but remember, they are just being what they are being. That they are doing it to us is not a truth. What they are being is independent of you. They would be the same way to someone else in your place. It is not personal, so it is best not to take it that way.

When a good friend of yours is having trouble in their life, you might find them curt, dismissive, or rude; because we know them and what is going on in their lives, we will be forgiving of them. We can do this because we do not take it personally. We know what the problem really is. In the case of a rude customer, we do not know what in their life is causing them to appear rude, so we assume that it is the way they are and that they are being rude to us, personally. This is most likely not true. It is the assumption we make that gets us into trouble. It is taking it personally that makes us feel badly when we encounter rude customers. To avoid this, I suggest a simple change in how we perceive the situation.

I know, easier said than done. This takes mindful practice and can take years to get good at. Once you begin practicing, you will also begin to see the benefits. People will no longer 'trigger' you into feeling a certain way. You maintain control of your internal state of being. You do not surrender your own personal power to someone you perceive as being rude 'to you.' This is why a job in the hospitality business is great training ground for learning this; you will encounter many more people in a day than most people. The chances of encountering a difficult customer are greater.

One morning, I came into the restaurant to find an employee crying in the back area and the supervisor very mad at the customer who 'caused' the problem. I found out what behavior had been and then went to speak to the customer. It was a Saturday morning, and it was not that busy, so I had a little more time for the customer than usual. Upon approaching the table and asking if there was anything I could do to help, I was immediately set upon regarding all that was wrong with my staff and my restaurant. Knowing that this outburst was not really about me, my staff, or the restaurant, I asked if I could sit at their table to discuss the problems. Mostly, I just listened. I knew from experience that this person just needed to be listened to, and I had time.

The customer continued to criticize everything from the staff's hair, the cleanliness of the bathroom, and even the pictures being crooked on the wall. She eventually got around to telling me that she had just been pink-slipped from a company she had worked for well over 20 years. She was very upset and taking it out on everyone and everything around her. Her companion was somewhat embarrassed, and I did my best to help with that as well. Once she had told me her story, she noticeably relaxed a bit, and I was able to offer something that would make her happy with her experience with us. I checked in on the table again a little later, and the customer was in better spirits.

When they were leaving, the customer waved me over, thanked me for being so gracious, and asked me to apologize to the staff for her earlier behavior. While we do not usually have time for that type of interaction, the point is that by remaining true to our offer of hospitality and not reacting negatively to her actions, I was able to turn a negative situation into a positive one. How? By not taking anything she said to me as personal. Because of that, I was able to remain centered and respond in a way that was hospitable.

We do not always have time to find out why someone is difficult or rude, but it often pays to remain centered and gracious in your response.

Of course, if I see and hear a customer treating any of our staff in a way that is inappropriate or abusive, I will intervene, and there have been times I have asked the customer(s) to leave. This goes back to treating my employees as my first line of customers. I must support and satisfy them every day. If I do not create a place where they feel safe and supported, I may lose them while attempting to take care of a rude customer and fail to attract the right employees in the future. This would create an unsustainable and ineffective business, and who needs that?

Quitting

"Life will only change when you become more committed to your dreams than your comfort zone." - Billy Cox

From a very young age, we are taught not to quit. We are taught that quitting is 'bad' and that we should never be a 'quitter.' Honestly, we are taught to 'stick it out' or 'hang in there'; we are told it will get better and that we must give it more time. We are inundated with success stories of people who do not give up and who do not quit. We see motivational quotes like this one from Walt Disney – "The difference is winning and losing is most often not quitting." And this one that I saw on a motivational poster - "It's always too early to quit." So, when it comes time to quit something, it is not surprising that people have mixed emotions about quitting and are not sure of the best way to go about quitting. A lot of this 'do not quit' rhetoric is about not giving up on your goals or dreams and is very valid, but the message is confusing to a young person who needs to quit something so they can pursue their goals. The truth is that quitting is a valuable skill to learn when one is pursuing their dreams.

Learning how to quit in an effective manner is an important skill to learn, as you will be doing it throughout your life. As you can imagine at this point, there is an effective way to quit something and a way that is ineffective for the future that you are working to create. There is no one right way to quit something because of the very many extenuating circumstances in every situation. There are, however, some basic ideas to guide you in quitting one job to move on to the next. For that matter, you can use the same basic ideas when quitting people, relationships, and unsatisfactory situations.

When thinking about quitting, keep the following things in mind. You must have a plan. You need to give adequate notice. You should take care of yourself and make sure you fulfill on your promises to others that will be affected. This is quitting with integrity, and integrity matters. Or, as the American businessman and author Harvey Mackay puts it, "If you have integrity, nothing else matters. If you don't have integrity, nothing else matters."

When quitting anything, you need to put yourself first because you are quitting to take care of you and the future you are working to develop. However, you must do so in a way that takes care of other people in the organization, be they co-workers, customers, managers, and the owners. Depending on the type of job and the level of responsibility you are entrusted with, you can give a minimum of two weeks' notice up to six months' notice. During your remaining time, you must always work up to the best of your ability and not slack off because you are leaving, as you may think that there are no consequences. Know that there are always consequences. Employers tend to remember your first few weeks on the job and your final few weeks on the job. If you want and/or need a good recommendation from your current job, it is best to be a rock star until your last day.

There are caveats to giving adequate notice to an employer. If you find yourself in a job or any situation where you are being abused, treated badly, or even where people are indifferent to you and your contribution, it is best just to leave. No notice needs to be given, as that is a courtesy, and if none is being shown to you, you do not have to return it. Cultural norms tell us we should give at least a two-week notice, but that is in a job where you are being treated fairly. If you are not being treated fairly, you do not have to be fair in return.

We start all our employees with a 30-trial period. We let them know that they can leave without notice inside of that 30 days if they find that they do not like the job. We have the same 30 days to decide if we believe that the employee can do the job and fits well with the culture. The hospitality industry is where many people get their first job. So, we not only have to help young employees navigate their first job, there are many times that we also must teach them how to quit.

As employees work to develop their careers, it is important to do so at a job that is right for them and their story of the future. If an employee feels that the job is not right for them, then they should just quit. Because if the job is not right for the employee, then the employee is most likely not right for the job. Another truth here is that this is your life, and you must take care the best way you can, even when it comes to quitting.

As you progress through your career, you will need to move from one job to another. By approaching quitting from a Selfishly Altruistic perspective, you can find a way that helps you to move on while also helping to take care of the people at the job you are leaving.

Learning how to quit is not just about leaving one job for another. We will sometimes find that we must quit our friends, relatives, and co-workers. You can do this without a formal announcement as you work to become a better version of yourself. Some people can just drag you down, and they do not care that they are doing so. To advance your career, you sometimes must quit co-workers and managers. You can still stay at your job, doing it because you love it and the satisfaction it brings, but you know that you will have to leave someday and always be looking for a strategic way out. I once had a run-in with the owner's wife at one job, and I just asked that if the owner wanted to communicate with me, he had to do it through the general manager. I was able to stay at a job I really enjoyed with employees who were great people to work with; I just quit dealing with the owners until the end of the season. I was able to do this without being fired because I was good at my job, and I made a difference in the workplace for customers and fellow employees. Essentially, I quit the owners and kept my job.

It is important to know that a business also needs to change. Losing employees is an important part of gaining new ones and opening new possibilities for the business. Some companies that experience low turn-over will make it a practice to remove the under-performing employees to always be hiring new people. New people in an organization are vitally important for the growth and direction of a company.

Quitting with integrity is a powerful move that helps you to achieve your goals. Quitting when things are bad is vital for your own well-being. Quitting when things are good so that you can advance your career is a Selfishly Altruistic move. When done effectively, everyone involved feels taken care of in a good way. Taking care in this way means people will speak well about you and your integrity. That has value for your future.

Have Fun!

"I am going to keep having fun every day I have left, because there is no other way of life. You just have to decide whether you are a Tigger or an Eeyore." - Randy Pausch

"It's fun to have fun, but you have to know how."
- Dr. Seuss

Have Fun, really. Why are you doing anything? Now, we all know it cannot be all fun and games all the time, but who is to say that it can't be fun most of the time? I know those pesky cultural and workplace pressures and norms. But I say, do not listen to that. Have Fun. Create the possibility of fun in your everyday life. Work with others to do the same. Help to create a place you want to work at each day.

In the restaurant industry, it is about fun. It is also creating a place with a sense of fun for the customer. We are in the hospitality industry, and so we work to create a place of hospitality. This includes comfort, quality, and pleasantness, all with an underlying sense of fun (except in the stuffiest of stuffy places). This must also be true for employees as well as customers. How can we create this space for customers if we are not feeling it ourselves? For most of my life as a manager of others, I have worked with the idea that my employees are my first-line customers. It is to them that I make the first promise of a satisfying and fun place to work. I need to create this place so it is possible. If this works well, then it will be easier to take care of my second-tier customers, the ones who come in with the money.

A sense of fun can be created by the top management. It can be created by the employees as well. But if the top management has a different mindset, it will be difficult but not impossible for employees to be completely successful. In all aspects of the service industry, a sense of fun must pervade. It is what most customers are looking for, and it helps employees experience job satisfaction.

In the jobs I have had, I always helped to create a sense of fun, within the confines of the job description and applicable laws. My mantra as an employee was, "If I can't have fun at work, why do the work?" This still holds true being self-employed and the owner of multiple restaurants. My job is to create a place where the 'right' employee shows up to work with us and is in sync with our story in the marketplace. If I create and tell this story well, then those who apply for a job with us will likely be the right fit for our place. When I was a teenager, the most concise version of my mantra was, "Have Fun. Learn things". This is still my essential mantra and one I share with our employees. I want them to show up in a good mood. I work to create the environment where they can have fun at work and still be very productive and an integral part of the team. This has worked for us for many years, and I expect it will work well throughout my working life.

There are many days at work that I feel that I am in a sitcom and that a sitcom based on our workplace would do well with the viewing public. Perhaps many people think that about their workplace. Maybe some people think of it more as a tragedy, but why work in a place like that? Funny things happen every day. From simple interactions with employees to complicated projects with vendors, some funny stuff happens that helps make the job fun and entertaining – stuff that makes for good stories and memories. Maybe one day I will write that sitcom. Every day there is a cast of characters that come through our doors, be it our front door, or the back door, or the Employee's Only door, or up from the basement.

Part 2 – Management

"To lead people, walk behind them."
- Lao Tsu

"The first responsibility of a leader is to define reality. The last is to say thank you. In between, the leader is a servant."
- Max De Pree

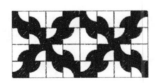

What is Management?

"When the best leader's work is done the people say, 'We did it ourselves.'" - Lao Tzu

Management of a business encompasses many areas of concern. What first comes to mind is the management of human resources (HR). HR is the largest expense for most companies and in most restaurants accounts for 30% - 35% of expenses. One part of HR management is controlling this expense, from what each person is paid, to the hours that are scheduled, to the management of staffing hours on a day-to-day basis. The other primary purpose of HR management is the hiring, education, and training of all employees. Most of HR management in our operation is controlled by the General Manager and the bookkeeper.

Management is defined as the organization and coordination of the activities of an enterprise in accordance with certain policies and toward the achievement of clearly defined objectives. Fundamentally, it is the organization of workflow and resources to effectively fulfill the company's offer.

Simply put, managers make requests of employees that fit inside the scope of the company's offer. Employees promise to fulfill these requests in a timely and effective manner to facilitate the smooth functioning of the business. This ensures satisfied customers, positive cash flow, and profitability. Essentially, managers must become proficient at making effective requests, and employees must become excellent at making and fulfilling promises.

A manager's other responsibilities include coordination of resources, maintenance of equipment, product flow (i.e., deliveries in and product out), product use, and efficiencies in all departments. Most importantly, this daily and weekly flow of inventories is the second largest expense in our business and subsequently an area where there can be substantial loss if not managed effectively.

This management of products in and out of the building is not too different than doing the same thing for your household, just on a much larger scale. In your own home, you go food shopping, cook food, and create meals, all while making an effort not to waste food or throw anything away. We bring in the raw product to the restaurant, turn it into something else, and then make sure that it leaves with the customer, all while mitigating waste. It is one of the main jobs on the kitchen manager in any restaurant. It takes a while to learn; it takes coordination with other employees and vendors and a certain skill in guessing the future. We call that making projections, and it is where budgeting falls under management. See the chapter on budgeting later in this book.

Managing others is a practice that you develop. It is not something you just know how to do. It is not just telling others what to do. Effective management has depth and meaning and takes care of the manager as well as what or who is being managed. What follows in this section are ideas and practices on management to help you have a better understanding of management.

Language is a Verb - Part 1

"Language is very powerful. Language does not just describe reality. Language creates the reality it describes." - Desmond Tutu

Grammatically language is not a verb. However, when used properly and with intent, language is the underlying power that shapes and moves our collective realities. Everything humans have created and shaped has been done because of our ability to use language as an effective tool for communication. This seems so obvious that it is almost a 'duh!' statement. My main point is that when language is used with intent, it has the most power. Cities get built, tunnels get dug, mountains get moved, all because someone first thought it was a good idea and then convinced others it was a good idea, all through the effective use of language. Declarations are made, requests are proffered, promises are given, and through all this, stuff happens, and things appear. The better you are at using your language, the more effective you will be in helping to co-create the world around you.

In a way, it is almost like magic. You cannot really see it until it is pointed out to you. It is so obvious it is invisible. Yet, it is the underlying cause agent of all that we as humans create. This includes giant projects like putting a man on the moon and personal projects that we engage in everyday life. Our world can only exist in and through language. If we do not have a word for something, it does not exist for us. This does not mean that it lacks objective existence; it just means that we cannot truly know of it or how it might impact our lives. We need a word to bring it into *our* existence.

The reason that you need to know this is so that you may understand what a powerful tool language is, especially for creating harmonious, effective organizations and work environments and for helping you to create your own life. In the book *The Four Agreements,* Don Miguel Ruiz has this to say: *"Be Impeccable With*

Your Word. Speak with integrity. Say only what you mean. Avoid using the word to speak against yourself or to gossip about others. Use the power of your word in the direction of truth and love." While he has much more to say about the power of "Your Word," this one quotation speaks powerfully about the integrity of language and habitual action we need in order to create the world we long to inhabit.

As a manager in any business, it is your job to bring forth the reality of the business for your employees. If you are the owner of a business, it is your job to bring forth the reality of the business for your customers and all its employees and vendors, this can only be done through language. I call it storytelling; many in business call it marketing. The business you create is constituted in language manifested as action. The more effective you can be daily with your words – in the shape of *requests, promises, declarations, assertions, assessments,* and *expressives* – the more effective you will be in creating and managing a successful business. We will cover more on these *speech acts* in the chapter on Language.

Throughout my career as an employee, I worked within other peoples' 'stories.' I had my own story of my life and how I wanted it to unfold, as did all my co-workers. But at the time, I had no idea that I was part of someone else's story. When I opened my first business with my family, we knew what our story was, and we worked to create it in the area where we were located. This story has constantly changed throughout our time in business, but it is mostly shaped by the words we use, the actions we engage in, and the story that unfolds from those actions. While there are many forces in play each and every day that help to shape our story, it is up to us to guide the story so that it works to create a profitable and enduring business – that takes care of its employees, its customers, and the community we live in. This can only happen with the effective use of language.

What does this mean for you? You also have this 'power.' Like any talent that you have, you must practice becoming proficient. This practice starts with your thoughts. It helps to develop positive and affirming thoughts about yourself and the life you want to create.

While this can be hard for some, it does get easier over time. What makes it difficult is that our bodies are emotion-and-thought-generating-machines. Experts estimate that the mind thinks between 60,000 – 80,000 thoughts a day. That is an average of 2,500 – 3,300 thoughts per hour. Other experts estimate a smaller number of 50,000 thoughts per day, which means about 2,100 thoughts per hour (there are different schools of thought on this - pun intended). Either way, that is a lot of thoughts. If you pay attention to these thoughts, you will discover that most of them are useless, unimportant thoughts that pass through the mind very quickly. There are words you repeat, comments the mind makes, repetitions of conversations, questions, answers, and many senseless meandering thoughts that you are probably not even aware that are just passing through. By taking the time to practice healthy and productive thoughts, you can begin to train your brain to be more effective in creating thoughts you actually want and can build upon.

This is the best reason to learn how to meditate. While that is not the onus of this book, I recommend that you begin to learn today. If you look, you will find ways to learn this practice on your own. A great way to start is to simply observe your thought process and practice letting go of all that arises. It is as simple as laying outside and watching the clouds go by and not thinking or obsessing about each cloud. Once you learn to let go of thoughts that do not serve you, you can focus on the thoughts that do serve you and the future you are working to build for yourself.

From our thoughts, we engage in conversations with our words. These conversations can turn into actions that serve to bring about the reality we all help to create in our everyday lives. We will cover more on this in the chapter about Telling Your Story later in this book, but suffice it to say, we have a great power if we choose to learn how to use language effectively.

Supportive Management

"As we look ahead into the next century, leaders will be those who empower others." - Bill Gates

When it comes to the daily operation of the restaurant, it is the manager's job to offer support for the employees who are working. As an effective manager, you should not be managing any employee directly unless they are new and still in training (or there is some new and immediate task that requires your direct work with an employee). Support and guidance are always the best and most effective ways to achieve your daily goals. You may have to move employees to specific jobs to manage the flow of service. You may have to 'jump in' to help an employee who needs extra help or to speed up service. It is usually during slow times that a manager's time is spent on extra management or simple direction. Prioritizing the workflow is the most important task during slow times. You will find that it is important during those slow times to control the costs by sending home the staff who are not needed. Occasionally you may have to guide the side and prep work to make the most efficient use of an employee's time. Having to 'manage' employees every day is tiresome and ineffective.

Support can take many shapes; it can be just being there to answer questions, all the way to working side by side on the line during busy times. Support can be finding and delivering items that an employee needs to fulfill their job requirements. Being present and listening is a great skill to develop. Support can sometimes mean guiding an employee toward tasks where they can be more productive or finding a way where an employee can be used more efficiently so they can experience more success as a worker and team member. It is certainly not productive for a manager simply to do the employee's work and not use the moment as a learning opportunity for the struggling employee. Mostly, you will be performing management by just being present.

This is leadership in the form of following. It is a very important skill to learn for just about any domain in which you find yourself. There are times that, as a leader, you will need to jump in and take control of a situation, but for the most part, good managers do not ever let it get to that point during the day. There is a saying that a manager's job is 'to put out fires.' I would say that only an ineffective manager's job requires that skill. An effective leader never lets the tinder and the spark get near each other to start a fire. What I mean is that an effective leader can look ahead and anticipate problems and do the work early on to prevent any problem from occurring or have an effective solution readily at hand. Effective managers often look like they are not even working because the work they do helps them mitigate breakdowns before they happen. This allows them to play a more supportive role throughout the day instead of fixing problems all the time.

Effective managerial support serves to create a teamwork approach that helps to mobilize employees into action. When they see that they are being supported in their daily jobs, they are much more willing to do the same for all other employees.

While I am working during a busy day, I may jump into 'dish-land' to help a newer employee get caught up with the pace at which the kitchen is operating. While I am there, I educate the employee to the effective practices that will provide more speed without sacrificing cleanliness. I always see that same employee do the same for a newer employee somewhere down the line; this type of support is a self-fulfilling prophecy. The more that each employee engages in the support of a fellow employee, the more that the desired supportive culture takes hold for the entire team; this is success by leading with support.

Plan on Problems
(Anticipate Breakdowns)

"It does not do to leave a live dragon out of your calculations, if you live near one." - J.R.R. Tolkien

Things go wrong. That is just how it is - every day. Expecting things to go wrong and being prepared to handle them in an effective manner is a skill that can be developed. I have often heard it said that a manager's job is to put out fires. A great manager's job is to make sure that a fire does not happen in the first place. If it looks like something will go wrong, the exceptional manager is prepared to work effectively with current resources to take care of the problem. Some examples include: employees will be sick, have a plan; equipment will break, have a plan; deliveries will be late, have a plan. Waiting around for something to go wrong and then not being prepared to handle it is ineffective management.

When I was learning to fly a single-engine plane, I learned that, as the pilot, I must always be anticipating engine failure and always looking for a place to land. Great pilots embody this knowledge and do it without even thinking about it. Great managers are the ones who anticipate problems and are always thinking about how to function if something goes wrong. They do not overdramatize a 'crisis' situation; they work efficiently with their resources to fix a problem and then move along smoothly with their day. Do not make breakdowns bigger than they must be by overdramatization. That is just managing from the ego. Those managers who, by their actions, say, "Look at me, aren't I great, I saved the day," are more driven by their need to be recognized than by their desire to be an effective manager. They will not be the manager who anticipates possible breakdowns and is prepared to fix them with minimal fuss and effort.

Planning anything, anywhere, you must plan for possible breakdowns and problems. You must think ahead and visualize as many situations as possible so you can have a plan and be prepared for the eventual problem when it arises. While it may not arise in the way you imagined it, you will be much more prepared to handle it because you prepared ahead of time. This works in all aspects of your life. From family vacations to simple day trips with friends. While I was never a Boy Scout, I understand that the Scout motto is, "Be Prepared," meaning that you are always ready to do what is necessary to help others. It also means you are ready, willing, and able to do what is necessary in any situation that comes along. It also means being prepared to take care of your future and the others you encounter along the way.

In the restaurant business, things go wrong just about every day. Whether they are mechanical failures, employee failures, sicknesses, schedule problems, quality concerns, you name it, if it can happen, it will happen. These are what we refer to as breakdowns. It is not so much the breakdown that is the problem; it is how we respond to the breakdown that makes the problem either bigger than it is or true to scale. Expecting that there will be breakdowns and being prepared for them to occur goes a long way toward mitigating these problems. It really starts with an accepting mindset. You must accept that problems are going to occur. You must accept them while they are happening. This puts you in a much better place to respond proactively, often with a premeditated solution. It sets you up to not be caught off guard and respond effectively and quickly to any given situation.

I often see people respond in ineffective ways to breakdowns. They fail to offer a timely and effective solution, and what they do offer turns out to be counterproductive. Many times, you will see people just get angry. They attempt to shift the blame to someone else, away from themselves and their lack of preparation for the situation. Attempting to find blame for a breakdown is not effective in the moment. What is effective is working to solve the immediate problem and take care of the situation in an effective manner. After the situation has been rectified and there is time, then you must investigate the breakdown – not to cast blame but with the desire to be prepared for the future. Casting blame is a useless waste of time and energy. Why? Because there is nothing actionable that comes from this behavior. Knowing what went wrong and who was involved is necessary, only to adjust for future situations. If an employee is involved in the same breakdown numerous times, it is time to take a different action.

People will often work to deflect blame in a breakdown. This is also unhelpful. Engaging in deflection does not fix a problem but makes you part of the problem, not the solution. Many people in the workforce, young and old, choose to deflect blame. How often have you heard this sentence: "It wasn't me" or "It wasn't my fault." Good managers and leaders do not care who did or did not cause a breakdown. They just want to fix it as soon as possible. Working to be a solution to a problem instead of part of the problem is a skill to develop. Being prepared is always the best thing you can do. Exceptional managers also want to reduce the possibility of the same breakdown in the future by pursuing a full understanding of the current situation.

In the hospitality business, there are plenty of good examples of breakdowns. Consider this scenario: the customer does not get what they ordered. Ineffective employees and managers will seek blame, deflect blame, and not fix the problem at hand. Effective employees and managers will seek to correct the problem by finding out what the customer was waiting for and then get it to them as quickly as possible. That is it. I often see people looking to blame someone or deflect blame and not engage in whatever action needs to be taken immediately to solve the problem. I am sure you can find many examples of this type of behavior in families, jobs, and even in schools. Be prepared and always work to fix the problem first. That is what is important.

Anticipating breakdowns is a skill that you can develop. Whenever you find yourself planning anything, it is always important to think of as many things that could go wrong and build an action plan that can help take care of them should they arise.

You can apply this type of thinking to your daily life. Breakdowns happen. What matters is how you respond, how well you have prepared, knowing that breakdowns happen. Fixating on who is to blame or trying to figure out when everything started to go wrong is unhelpful. Again, what matters is how you have prepared yourself to handle whatever may be happening in the moment. If you are prepared, you do not get angry, you are not looking to cast blame, you accept it for what it is, you make the necessary changes, you take the required action, and you move forward toward a solution. Do what you can to take care of yourself, be prepared, and work to take care of breakdowns in an effective manner. Always be open to learning something new in these situations.

Winograd, Terry, and Fernando Flores. *Understanding Computers and Cognition: A New Foundation for Design*

Language: What Are We Doing?

"Watch your thoughts, they become words;
watch your words, they become actions;
watch your actions, they become habits;
watch your habits, they become character;
watch your character, for it becomes your destiny.
    -Frank Outlaw

With our millions of words, all that we are attempting to do with language can be summed up in five words. I know, 'no way!' But think about it. Think of anything you have said or will possibly say – or what you have heard others say, either to you or anyone else. Try to find something that does not fit with one or more of the following five Linguistic Acts.

    1. Directives or Requests
    2. Commissives or Promises
    3. Declarations
    4. Assertives or Assessments
    5. Expressives – express a psychological state about a state of affairs ("I am sorry")

Directives or Requests – get the listener to do something, as in "please do this...."

Commissives or Promises – commit to some future course of action as in "I will do that..."

Declarations – declaring something new as true as in "I now pronounce you man and wife."

Assertives or Assessments – commit the speaker to something being the case as in "I have completed the task you set for me."

Expressives – express a psychological state about a state of affairs as in saying "I am sorry" or "that is a nice tie."

The above information on Speech Acts comes from the book *Understanding Computers and Cognition: A New Foundation for Design* by Terry Winograd and Fernando Flores. I have found this understanding of language put forth in this book to be very beneficial in the management of a business.

Perhaps you wonder why you need to know this. It is because language – whether as spoken or written words or as body language or gesture – is how we communicate our ideas to others. By knowing the five basic "acts" or actions of language, we can better understand what others are trying to say to us. We can create more effective language strategies for conveying our ideas to others. Remember, language is the way we co-create our world together.

In the work environment, two of the above actions recur most often. They are requests (Directives) and promises (Commissives). We use all the others as well, but making requests and fulfilling promises is what the workplace is all about. The better you are at making requests and fulfilling promises – skills we can learn – the more effective manager or new hire you will become. We are going to learn more about promises and requests in a later chapter. But first, we need to learn about the skill of listening. Otherwise, those requests go in one ear and out the other.

Listening as a Skill

"The most important thing in communication is hearing what isn't said" - Peter Drucker

It may come as no surprise, but we are not taught how to learn to become good listeners. This inability to listen is in a significant oversight in our school system with its lack of classroom instruction on learning the skills of a good listener. Our schools have focused attention on reading, considering it to be the main way in which we learn. We have practically forgotten the art of being a good listener. In our current school systems, about six years are devoted to formal reading instruction. There is little emphasis placed on speaking, and almost no time or attention is given to developing listening as a skill. This is odd since there is so much lecturing done in college. Our students are not prepared to learn because of their lack of training in how to listen well. Our way of training people how to listen has often consisted merely of a series of directives extending from the first grade through high school where students are told to "Put your listening ears on!" "Pay attention!" or "Listen up!" and many other short directives.

While there should be a chapter on listening in the employment section of this book, I want to focus more attention on this topic here. Quite frankly, I was not the best listener as an employee and would often get just enough information to not get into trouble. It did not help that my managers were not good at making requests either. Most people do not even know that they have not developed the skill of becoming a good listener. Attempting to inform them that they do not listen well will fall on deaf ears (pun intended). I began to learn how to become a better listener as a young manager. It was expected of me as an employee, but I was not as good as they thought, nor are most young people.

As a manager, it is imperative that we make good requests. Built into the construct of those requests is your understanding of the promisor, who in this context is also the listener. It is important to know that the person to whom you are speaking can hear what is being requested, understand the scope of the request, make sense of what is being asked in the context of where the request is being made and then be able to act to fulfill on that request; this is a tall order. What is essentially happening is that the requester is taking their thoughts and putting them into words. Those words are broadcast through the power of speech into the air to the listener, who hears the words and then must reassemble them into thoughts that they can effectively use to take action. It is kind of like taking down a barn piece by piece, loading it onto a truck, and moving it to another state, and then having someone else reconstruct the barn without any schematics because they know what a barn looks like. As you can see, there is lots of room for error.

To make matters worse, we can think much faster than we talk. The average human speaks at about 125 words per minute, which is much slower than the brain needs to process those words. When we listen, we ask our brains to receive words at an extremely slow pace compared to their capabilities. To put it another way, we can listen and still have some spare time for thinking. This leaves room for more to go wrong, as the listener's untrained brain will start to wander.

The real problem when making requests happens when we spend too much time talking. When making requests, it is best to keep them short and direct. However, a manager's job goes beyond making requests. We often must educate people and take time to teach them new aspects of a job. When we take the time to educate a person on a new job or task, we can help them listen better by helping them use their spare thinking time efficiently as they listen. You can do this by stopping and checking in often and have them summarize what you have been speaking about. You can also ask the person to think about the validity of what is being taught and if it resonates with their current thinking and understanding. Stop often and allow them to ask questions. A conversation about a new job is much easier to process than a lecture.

As I mentioned earlier, I was not a very good listener as a young person. I spent far too much time talking and not enough time listening in a meaningful way. It was not until my mid-twenties that I started to think that I needed to develop the skill of listening. It was after someone misquoted a saying by Plato to a group of people I was talking 'at.' This is not exactly what was said, but it had the same meaning, "Wise men speak because they have something to say; Fools because they have to say something." After that I decided to become a better listener and to pay more attention and show more of a genuine interest to the people around me.

I began to deepen my listening skills further after taking a business class based in biology. Many people find difficulty in accepting that humans are still biologically animals. We are a species of primate-Homo sapiens that can walk on two legs and happens to have an advanced brain. But like any other species, we are still dominated by biological rules that control our actions, reactions, body language, and gestures. Understanding this as a foundation in a business class was very revealing. Learning how to listen with more than just my ears was extremely helpful. Of course, we all do this automatically, being biological creatures, and we only are aware to a certain degree of body language. Learning to understand it and develop it as a skill was something else entirely.

Albert Mehrabian, a researcher of body language, first broke down the components of a face-to-face conversation. He found that communication is 55% nonverbal, 38% vocal, and 7% words only. While it is impossible to say this is an absolute truth, what is essential to know about this is that nonverbal communication happens all the time. We can learn to pay attention and 'listen' to that part of communication, as well as in our daily interactions. Reading body language is like learning a second language and can help you understand a given situation more effectively. While everyone does this with various levels of understanding, working to improve upon it will help in your conversations with others in all aspects of your life.

One of my employees came to the office one day to voice her concerns about working with another employee. This is something that we ask them to do, and we find that the more we know about all the employees, the better we are at building teams of people that work well together. After listening to her and paying attention to her social, historical self and the context in which she came to speak to me, I was able to speak to her about more than that one issue. Together we came up with a plan that would help her and others in the place as well. When she was leaving, she turned and asked me how it is that I know so much. I replied that it was just magic. But of course, it is not just magic; like a good fortune teller, I listen to what is happening around me. This from the New York Times about fortune tellers: "Research into the fortune-telling business shows that operators use a technique known as 'cold reading,' which can produce an accuracy of around 80 percent when 'reading' a person you've never met. While it can appear to be magical to naive and vulnerable people, it is simply a process based on the careful observation of body language signals plus an understanding of human nature and a knowledge of probability statistics." See, not magic. And mine is not 'cold reading' because I know the person in front of me.

Learning to pay fuller attention to more than just the words that were coming out of someone's mouth helped to shape my own listening skills and, at the same time, it helped to sharpen my intuition. I worked at becoming a proficient listener as I started to pay more attention to all the intangibles in our culture. When I listen to someone, I do not just listen to the words they are saying. I also 'listen' to the situation, the social and historical culture, and the context in which the conversation is taking place. Then I pay attention to as much of that background as possible. I pay attention to the pauses, the space where there are no words. I will ask, 'Why is this person saying what they are saying? What is it about who they are in this place and time that has them expressing their ideas/concerns to me at this moment?' I listen with all my senses. I pay attention to body language as well as vocal inflections and attempt to 'feel' what is being transmitted. It is a lot, but I have been able to appear to 'read the minds' of my employees because I have developed such good listening skills. They will often say to me, "How do you know that?" I let them know that it is because I am a good listener. It also helps that I have worked with the same age group of employees since I was their age group, and I have a good and evolving understanding of their concerns.

As a manager of people, one of the best skills you can develop is your ability to listen well. It becomes a *secret skill* of sorts because most people will not be able to discern what you are doing and how you are able to understand and know so much. What you will be doing is becoming an *active listener*. Taking an interest in your employees beyond their work-life will help you get a better understanding of their concerns. You will be in a better position when it comes time to help them become more effective in their jobs and roles.

Active listening at work is critical if you are in a management position or interact with co-workers. Active listening allows you to understand problems and collaborate to take care of customers and solve problems. It also reflects your patience, a valuable skill in any workplace. Note that this takes lots of practice. I often find times when I am not engaged in active listening, and it will tend to cause breakdowns. I have to recognize that it was my failure and not shift the blame to the person talking to me.

In the hospitality industry, listening to customers' concerns is also very valuable. While we do not often have the time to be as attentive as we may like due to the fast-paced nature of the work, I have found that when I have the time, listening to a customer who has a complaint or concern goes a long way in resolving the situation. This is also true when it comes time to listen to my employees. Taking the time to really listen to an employee's concern or complaint is crucial to gaining a full understanding of any situation. It also gives the employee time to be 'heard,' and that is often enough. There are many times that I have taken an employee who is upset about something to a quiet place and just let them express what is bothering them. Often in putting their thoughts and feelings into words they come up with their own solutions. Making time for this also allows me as the manager to have a better understanding of the employee as well as the situation. That just leads to better and more effective management. It is managing from a place of care, that manifests itself as effective listening.

I know we do not always have that kind of time to listen to someone, but if you do have the time, the results will be much better. Active listening takes time to learn. Here are a few things to keep in mind when you are practicing this type of listening:

- Make eye contact while the other person speaks. It also helps to lean toward the other person and nod your head occasionally.
- Paraphrase what has been said, rather than offering unsolicited advice or opinions. Make an effort not to interrupt while the other person is speaking.
- Do not spend time thinking about your reply while the other person is speaking; the last thing that he or she says may change the meaning of what has already been said.
- Watch for nonverbal behavior to pick up on hidden meaning, in addition to listening to what is being said. Watch facial expressions, listen to the tone of voice, and pay attention to other behaviors that can sometimes tell you more than words alone.
- As best you can turn off your internal dialogue while listening or direct it to the conversation at hand. It is quite difficult to attentively listen to someone else and your own internal voice at the same time.
- Show interest by asking questions for clarification.
- Be open, neutral, and work at withholding judgment while you are listening. Note that you may agree or disagree, but do not act on those assessments in a harmful way.

- Be patient while you listen. As I noted before, we can listen much faster than another can speak.

Active listening is also something you can teach to your employees. By teaching this, you will deepen your own understanding and skill. This ability will come in handy as you develop your own career and will make yourself a valuable member of any team. This is also important in all your relationships. It will help diminish misunderstandings that happen from time to time.

Promises and Requests

"Promises are the uniquely human way of ordering the future, making it predictable and reliable to the extent that this is humanly possible." - Hannah Arendt

Promises and Requests are two of the five Linguistic Acts in which humans engage in. These two are crucial for business because this is where language turns into action. Managers require employee action to fulfill the business's offer.

Let us start by taking a closer look at promises. Most people, when asked, will say that they rarely break promises. I say that most people make promises they do not even realize they are making and subsequently break them regularly. In the workplace, employment is a conditional promise. A conditional promise is simply, 'I will do this for you if you do this for me.' An employer promises to pay employees in a timely and fair manner. They may also make other promises such as: reimbursed education, health insurance, clean work environment, etc. An employee promises to work for the employer and fulfill all the employers' requests as they relate to the specific job. There are many specified requests in a workplace, and if there is an Employee Handbook and/or Reference Manual, these requests are spelled out. There are many unspecified or implicit requests that are part of any particular job. Some examples of these may include: being on time, working well with others, being in a good mood, keeping a clean and safe workplace, and treating others with courtesy and respect. There can be any number of implicit requests in any workplace. These implicit requests, what I call promises, are what employees (and employers) will often overlook and wind up breaking.

I have found it essential as a manager to make all implicit requests in an explicit form. Or, to put it another way, I explain (make explicit) every possible request that I may think employees ought to 'know' because it is part of my business's 'common sense.' I will talk about this in greater depth later in the book.

When I hire an employee, I make it very explicit that I am promising to pay them for showing up on time and being in a mood of willingness. For many if not all employers, this mood of willingness is implied. I make it explicit. If it is not there on a given day, they must get into a mood of willingness or go home for the day. If they must go home, I make it very clear to all remaining employees why their co-worker is not there. Many of them do not mind the extra workload since it means they are also free of a bad, and often infectious, attitude or mood.

A promise is a statement or commitment that tells someone, that you will either do something or that something will happen, or it is an assurance of some future success, change, or improvement. Employees promise to fulfill the Conditions of Satisfaction listed in the Employee Handbook and Reference Manual, along with all other requests as they are made and are relevant to the job description. A manager's job is to become proficient at making effective requests and helping to create an environment where good promisors can thrive.

A request is an act of politely or formally asking for something. A manager who makes a request assumes that the employee who promises to fulfill the request is willing and able to do so. But are you putting the request to the right person, at the right time, in the right way? Does the employee possess an adequate knowledge to fulfill the request? If something goes wrong, it is generally at the request level that a breakdown begins to happen. As a manager, it is important to learn how to make direct and effective requests to the right people.

The manager's job function is to help employees keep their promises with reminders, encouragement, and gentle direction. If you find that you always must direct the same employee (i.e., 'manage' them), it may be time for the manager to have a discussion with that employee. Once an employee has been trained and educated in all the aspects of their job, they should not have to be directly managed on a daily basis. You have more important things to do than to directly manage employees. Education and training are crucial elements to employees being able to function effectively in a work environment without direct and immediate supervision. Yes, you will have to oversee and guide the workflow of each day, but the direct management of each employee should not be required. By adopting an effective management style, we create employees that are autonomous with most of their daily actions.

Very simply, managers make requests, and employees say 'yes' to requests, promising to fulfill them. The crucial request found in our Employee Manual – which aims to ensure that promises get fulfilled – is that employees show up in a mood of willingness. See more about this in the section entitled "The Yes Path."

Explicit vs. Implicit

"Once you communicate, you don't discover reality, you create reality." - Meir Ezra

Engaging in effective communication is how managers get things done. The better we are with our requests, the better the outcome. The main problem in most requests (conversations about achieving coordinated action to achieve a desired outcome), is that there are a lot of implied requests and not enough explicit requests. In other words, there is a lot left unsaid in the original request, which causes ambiguity and basic miscommunication. To make matters worse, we often make requests speaking to what we assume is an employee's common sense. Unless you as the manager/requester have taken the time to build and cultivate the range of common sense you expect among the employees, then you are speaking to something that does not exist. This is true for other domains other than work, like family or community.

Common sense is only common to a subset of people in any population. For example, there is a common sense among doctors, but there are different ranges of common sense from one hospital to another. In any working environment, you need to learn that environment's common sense so you can coordinate effectively with everyone else. Inside any one hospital, there are common sense differences between departments. Effective communication from a common understanding is vitally important.

If you are a business owner or manager, it is your responsibility to build this common sense. It is also your job to see to it that your employees learn the common sense of the place where you manage. Common sense must be learned; it is not what most people think that it is (i.e., common to all).

The point here is that if you are making requests of people and relying on a common sense that you only believe exists, then you will encounter numerous breakdowns.

Make as much as you can explicit in your work environments, as well as in other areas where you coordinate with others to achieve desired outcomes. Use your language to create the common sense that people can effectively work with and around. If there are things that are implied in a request, take the time to make these things explicit. The best way to do this is in writing and by publishing an Employee Manual or by updating an existing Employee Manual. It does not even have to be a manual. It could be in the form of a story that specifies areas of coordinated action and highlights the 'things' we coordinate around to get the job done. It can be in posters, like safety posters. It can be in the form of weekly employee meetings where we use the same language and often revisit topics of discussion. There are countless ways to use language to create a common sense. The important thing is to make the many implied requests into explicit requests.

For example, I often use the simple request of taking out the garbage to illustrate this concept. In a restaurant, there are many locations where garbage is stored before removal from the building. The full request would look something like this, "Please take out all the garbage in the building, including the kitchen, the dining room, and the bathrooms. Clean any garbage can that needs to be cleaned, and do not forget that you also must take out all the recycling. Then you must clean the area around the dumpsters. Then you have to replace all the garbage bags with the appropriately sized can liners." A manager will not be making that kind of request every day. They will just say, "Please take out all the garbage and recycling." You can see that in the second iteration of the request, there is a lot implied in the request that requires specific knowledge. This knowledge is the common sense that is created in a work environment. It needs to be taught. It needs to be embodied by all the employees. Much of this will happen in the general training and education on the job, but it is important to be as explicit as possible when doing that education and training. Having the job fully explained in a work manual goes a long way toward helping to create this desired common sense.

Another good example from the restaurant would be the use of in-house recipe books. I learned this the hard way. When we opened our first restaurant, we did not use recipe books. There were only a few people making the staple recipes, so the recipes did not need to be written down. As we grew, we had to have more employees who knew how to make our staple offerings. We did what we call 'verbal it,' i.e., tell them the recipe and expect them to follow it. Boy, was that ineffective. It only took a few times for me to notice employees putting uncalled for seasonings in a recipe for me to make an attempt to fix the problem. The recipes were implied. They were not explicit. It took a lot of time, but we created what today is a 120-page recipe book. That being said, the recipe book is still taken out and updated based on changes in availability, pack size, and other factors that can affect a recipe.

In the restaurant industry, one of the things we sell is consistency. Customers want the item they had last week to taste like the item they are having this week. This is true in most businesses, as customers like the comfort of consistency. Think about your daily habits and purchases. I am guessing you often go to the same places and order the same things: the same gas station, the same clothing store. These places are consistent because, at the management level, their internal requests are explicit with little that is implied or left up to the 'common sense' of the employees fulfilling those requests.

So, look around in the different areas of your life. Do you see where breakdowns and mistakes are happening because there is too much implied and not enough being made explicit? It is important in any relationship to understand the common sense that other people might possess. It is important to build a common sense together. In my marriage, there are many times when there is not enough information to coordinate action effectively; this is true in most relationships. Take the time to gather the necessary information, make explicit the implicit, and work toward more effective communication.

Understanding other people's styles of communication is also important. I refer to what I call 'spouse speak.' It seems to be common when I talk with other couples about the phenomenon. Many spouses will phrase a request as a statement. It took me a few times to learn this way of communicating, and I have become pretty good at fulfilling requests that are hidden inside the statement. Here are a few examples:

The bird feeder is empty = Please feed the birds.
The garbage is full = Please empty the garbage.
The children will be ready at 5:00 pm = Please pick up the children at 5:00 pm.
The cat just came in = Please check the cat for ticks.

I mention this mostly for fun, but the importance of learning how to communicate with other people is vital for creating coordinated action. As Don Miguel Ruiz says in the book *The Four Agreements*, "Be impeccable with your words." Be impeccable with your understanding as well.

Managing Promises

"Sometimes people do not understand the promises they're making when they make them." - *John Green*

Exceptional managers do not manage people; they manage promises. Managing people is a pain in the ass and requires a lot of time and attention. If you find yourself in a position of managing people, you need to develop a meaningful way to switch from managing people to managing their promises.

A real-world example of this is how we work to manage the promise of being on time for work. We had a manager work for us who had previous management experience at a regional chain restaurant where they would write up employees for being late. So, this manager would wait for employees who were late and then give them verbal warnings when they arrived; this was his way of trying to manage the employee. It was totally counterproductive. We have an employee who is running late and most likely feeling stressed about that. Now we cause further stress when they arrive. Then we tell them to go in and be friendly to co-workers and customers. It took a few months, but I was able to get him to work it differently so that he was managing the implicit promise the employee made by accepting a job – be on time.

When an employee is running late, all we ask is for a phone call or a text to let us know. That is it. When they arrive, we check in with them to see if they are ok. If they apologize to us, we tell them that they do not owe us an apology. After all, they just saved us some money in payroll. They need to apologize to their co-workers; they had to pick up the slack because the employee was late. The promise they make is to be on time for their co-workers, not the management. We let them know that we do not really care if they are late. They can be late all they want. Just let us know, so we are not wasting time trying to get your shift covered. However, if your co-workers come to us and complain about chronic lateness, then we must listen to them. Our promise to everyone is to hire and maintain quality employees who keep their promises. That is managing promises and not the employee.

Most people do not even know that they are making promises daily. In a work environment, most of the promises that employees make are implicit; the promises they are making are implied as part of the job. Many of the jobs I had in my teens and early twenties came with little instruction and almost no education from the employer. They were relying on my 'common sense' to know the job and do my best. This way of 'teaching' can work for some people. It is a disservice to many, as I experienced with my co-workers in those years. If specific instructions were not given, many employees would choose to do nothing.

In contrast, I always had the ability to see the larger picture. I was able to keep working without direction, often beginning and completing tasks that were not assigned to me, mainly because I could see that they needed to be done. My experience has taught me that this is not the way many employees work.

Do not get me wrong; I did my share of slacking when I could, and I fully understand the need for employees to have some downtime, especially when we are in our busy season. There were a few times that I took a little longer in the bathroom just to get a break from the pace of the day's business. There were times I took a little longer on a job so I would not have to start a new one right away or on the same day. As an owner/manager, I still take this downtime when it is needed. Some days I get little done, and that is okay. It is important to recognize this in employees and give them the downtime that they will need.

By making the important requests explicit, I have found that it is much easier to help employees manage their promises and avoid having to manage each employee every day. Making these requests and promises explicit is just making them part of your story, part of your business's common sense. We do this in many ways: through an Employee Manual, employee meetings, written communications, texts, and through one-on-one meetings with employees. By these means of communication, I make explicit the implicit in our relationship.

The whole first section of this book gives examples of how we do this. Our job as managers is to engage in this over and over until it becomes the 'common sense' or 'acquired sense' of our workplaces. When employees know what is expected of them (the requests) and they are reminded that their work fulfills the promises that they have made by being an employee, then they are consistently able to fulfill on those promises. Through their employment, they are making promises, first and foremost to themselves and the future value that they are creating. They are then making promises to their customers that they will fulfill the company's offer. Another important promise they are making is to their fellow co-workers; they are saying, "Hey, your jobs just got easier because I am here." All employees rely on each other to create a fun and fulfilling work environment. Finally, the employees are making a promise to the employer to help fulfill the company's offer and to help the business become a profitable and enduring company. All these requests and promises need to be made explicit, and employees need to be reminded of the promises they are regularly making.

I find that it is much easier to remind an employee of their promises than it is to manage them on an ongoing and daily basis. I often tell employees who have been with us for six months or more that if I must manage them, it means I must get rid of them. An employee's job is to learn all that needs to be done and then do it because it builds their own story about what they are becoming. Employees that are not able to work in this way are not a fit for our company. We will always work with them to help them to be a fit until we need to help them learn how to quit. Oddly enough, quitting is something that is not taught in our culture. I could devote a whole chapter to learning how to quit well (I did, it is in the previous section). Quitting, when done right, is mutually beneficial. Also, I have found that when we must fire an employee, it should be done in a mutually beneficial way. While this cannot always be the case due to extenuating circumstances, it can be a great learning experience for all involved. I told one of my managers that there would come a time when an employee she had to fire will come back to say thank you. She came to me and told me the first time that happened to her. This is when we understand the deeper meaning behind firing an employee in a mutually beneficial way.

Early in my management experience, I would often conduct exit interviews with employees and managers. During one such interview, I asked a manager what she did not like about the job. She said, "I do not like telling the same people to do the same thing over and over again." At that time, I told her that, it is one of the main jobs of a manager and that if she were not doing that, I would not need her as a manager. Later, I thought more about what I had said to her and realized that it was the culturally accepted definition of a manager's job. I then set out to create a manager's position that did not include that as the main job description. Through my continued education and refinement of the workplace, I was able to create a story that did not have, "telling the same people the same thing over and over again" as a main part of the job. Do not get me wrong, we are not performing magic here; that part did not go away entirely, but we were able to mitigate it substantially.

We do this by creating a place where people want to work. We create a fun environment that helps them take care of themselves while taking care of the customer and their co-workers. The job is as much about their future as it is about maintaining an enduring business. We create a story that mobilizes an employee into action. It is much easier to remind a mobilized employee about their promises than it is to manage an unmotivated employee. Either you will make an effort to engage the unmotivated employee, or you will need to get rid of them. Build the team you want to be around and have around you.

Early on, I told one of my partners that his main job was to create a team of people around him that he wanted to be around. If he came into work and saw an employee that made him groan inwardly, it was time to take action to help that employee become a motivated,

112

mobilized employee, one the partner wanted to see and work with every day, or he had to get rid of that employee. If he found it difficult to work with an employee, it was most likely true for many of the staff. For many years, this partner did not take my advice and often put up with substandard employees who often brought the entire team down; he was creating an environment even he did not want to be in. Eventually, he came to realize that if he surrounded himself with people he genuinely liked and wanted to be around, then most likely everyone else would genuinely like working together. Creating an effective and caring team starts at the top.

Believe me, this does not always work. A lot depends on the employee's own declaration, or lack thereof. I spent years working with people who were not in a declaration of improving and/or needing help. I caused more than one problem by making an effort to help an employee who was not asking for help. I would spend time and energy on an employee I thought could be a more effective member of the team. Often, this has backfired on me, and I found that the rest of the employees suffered with this employee while I was trying to 'help' them when they had made no declaration for help. Making the right assessment of an employee and asking them if they want the help you can offer, I have found, is crucial. I let a lot of my employees down by working with an employee I should have fired. It took a long time to learn that lesson, as my tendency is to offer help. I had to realize that I was doing more damage than good to the rest of my staff.

Once you have created an effective team of people and have crafted an honest and compelling story that attracts the right employees and customers, it is much easier to manage promises than it is to manage employees, freeing a manager up to take the time to effectively manage the business like a high-performance sports team rather than a kindergarten class.

The 'Yes 'Path - Part 2

"The art of communication is the language of leadership."
- James Humes

The 'Yes' Path is also known as the 'Happy Path.' Why? Because when we all follow it, all our interactions run smoothly, and the business day flows seamlessly. The 'Yes' Path is simply the diagram of Promises and Requests made in any conversation that results in action. In the world of work, it is the flow from (A) a manager's request to (B) an employee's fulfillment of the employee promise to (A) the manager's declaration of satisfaction on the job's completion. For example:

A: Manager: "Take out all the trash and let me know when you have finished."
B: Employee: "Yes, I will take care of that."
B: Employee: "I have finished."
A: Manager: "Great job, thank you."

Requests are not just made by employers to employees. Business owners also make them to their vendors, managers to managers, employees to employees, etc. Anywhere there is an action that needs to be completed, there is a requester and a promisor. Knowing that and acting with that knowledge will help you to become a more effective requester.

The diagram below shows what we refer to as the 'Yes' Path. This diagram is part of a larger diagram that is called the Basic Conversation for Action and shows in graphical form what can happen in a conversation when a request is made. The 'Yes' Path is the line across the top. An employee's job is to say 'yes' to requests (in a mood of willingness). A manager's job is to make (effective) requests. Many things can go wrong when making requests, from badly phrased requests to requests made of the wrong people. Most of the time, if a request is not taken care of effectively, it is most likely the request itself that caused the breakdown.

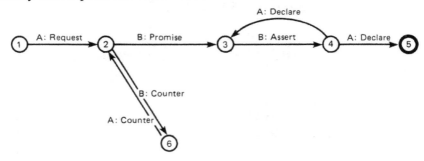

Figure 5 – The "Yes" Path with Counter

In the diagram above, the arrow from 4-3 listed as 'A: Declare,' is where the manager can say that the job was not completed and specifies what else needs to be done. Using the same example with the removal of the trash, the manager could Declare, "You forgot the bathroom garbage." At which point, the employee will take care of that part of the request and Assert that the job has been completed.

There is a caveat to the 'Yes' Path. The employee gets to say, "Yes, but...." The reason behind this is that the manager cannot possibly know all that an employee is engaged in at any given time. An employee may be working on something more important than the immediate request from the manager. So, the employee gets a chance to tell the manager what they are engaged in, at which point the manager may override or reassign that job request or withdraw the request completely and make the request of another employee. In the diagram above, this is the section called Counter that goes from 2 – 6. There is more to the Basic Conversation for Action than the one pictured above. If you are a manager of people, you should take the time to study and understand the whole diagram that is pictured below.

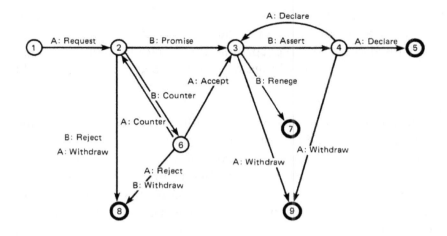

Figure 6 – The Basic Conversation for Action

It is important that managers learn to make effective requests. Most of the time, when a request is not taken care of effectively by an employee, it is because there was a problem with the request. We work with our managers to reflect on requests that they have made and find ways to improve on their requesting skills. In the following quotation attributed to Aristotle, we can replace the words 'become angry' with the words 'make requests'; it makes sense and deepens the point I am making:

ARISTOTLE: *"Anybody can become angry - that is easy, but to be angry with the right person and to the right degree and at the right time and for the right purpose, and in the right way - that is not within everybody's power and is not easy."*

JESSURUN: *"Anybody can make requests - that is easy, but to make requests with the right person and to the right degree and at the right time and for the right purpose, and in the right way - that is not within everybody's power and is not easy."*

The requester must consider who the promisor is and to what degree they can even fulfill the request. The requester must also consider the current situation, the current time frame, and many other factors. A manager who is effective at making requests has worked hard to become so and, as Aristotle points out, it is not easy. Making requests is a practice, one that you can become proficient at over time with attention and a deepening understanding of language and how we use it to make things happen to create our shared world space.

The problem that we encounter in our culture is that we like to blame the promisor, which does not lead us to an effective fix of the main problem. If you do not identify the problem correctly, you cannot fix the problem. We all too often blame the promisor when the problem is with the requester. The more that managers can recognize this, the better they will be at working on themselves to become more proficient at making requests. Their proficiency will result in enabling the whole team to be able to stick to the 'Happy Path.'

Believe me, I was not good at this as a young manager. I had no idea of this concept and would simply do what I learned from my culture and the workspaces in which I found myself. I was often an ineffective manager who did not take responsibility for my own ineffectiveness. Oddly, it went mostly unnoticed by everyone because that was the way everyone saw the world. It was only after learning the hard way (you know that way), that I became more effective in enhancing my own abilities.

More on Who Do You Work For?

"Studies indicate that happy employees are more productive, more creative, and provide better client service. They're less likely to quit or call in sick. What's more, they act as brand ambassadors outside the office, spreading positive impressions of their company and attracting star performers to their team." - Ron Friedman

Earlier, we looked at the *Who Do You Work For* circle from the employee's perspective. Here I want you to think about it from the manager's perspective and from your whole life perspective. I have put the graphic below, so you do not have to refer to the one earlier in the book. Besides, seeing and engaging with ideas repeatedly will help them to become embodied knowledge.

Who Do You Work For? If your answer does not include yourself and the future you are working to create, as well as the customer, your co-workers, and the owners/managers who make your job possible, then you should go back and refresh. This idea is the basis of what is called Selfish Altruism. I apply this type of outlook and behavior to the workplace because it just makes sense to me. My hope is that it makes sense to you, too.

We need to embody this knowledge and then work from this perspective. You need to teach this to your employees. You want to create an environment where you put them first. When employees feel that they are being well taken care of, they will strive to do their best because it just makes sense. Or, as a college student put it to me after I presented in her classroom, "If everyone at my job worked this way, work would be easy for everyone." Yup.

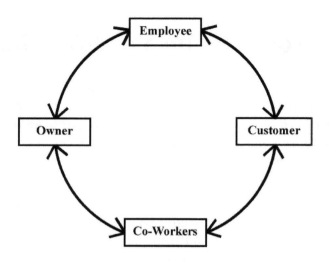

Figure 7 – Who Do You Work For?

When you can approach your work life from this perspective, this is where your understanding of this concept goes from understanding to embodied knowledge. This is what will help you to develop a workplace where people want to be and work in. We have been using this idea since the beginning of The Vanilla Bean Café, and while it has been refined over the years, it is still the same idea. We have not put an ad in the paper or on the internet for help since 1996. The right people just show up. I call it self-selecting. We create a place that is spoken about in the marketplace as a good place to work. We put the employee first, and we live it every day. Our turnover rate is one of the lowest in the industry. We keep employees for 3-5 years with some even reaching the 10-year mark. That is very rare in the fast-casual restaurant environment.

As a manager, if you are working for yourself every day and working to create a happier, more valuable you in your future, you will be able to teach this to your employees. Your job is to create a place where the right people self-select and show up. How? Because they became aware of your story in the marketplace. This makes the human resources part of a manager's job much easier, which means that you get to spend more time on other tasks that are beneficial to the future of the business and to you.

It *IS* About the Employee!

"Leadership is not about being in charge. Leadership is about taking care of those in your charge." - Simon Sinek

The title of this chapter says it all. It IS about the employee. If your employees are sixteen to about twenty-two years old, you will find the world is all about them. They are in the age of discovery and working to find where they fit in the world. To them, it is about them. So, it only makes sense to create a place, to create a narrative that speaks to where they are inside their skin. When you do this, they will engage with you in a much more effective way.

If you work with older people, this still goes a long way toward employee satisfaction. Make a point each day to engage an employee about what is going on in their lives and find a way to connect that back to the work they are doing or the field in which they work.

Creating a place where the employee feels valued and cared for goes a long way toward creating a great place to work and a profitable, enduring company where you want to spend your days.

If you genuinely care about your employees because it is what you genuinely want to do, the level of care you exude will return to you, and you will find that you are doing this for yourself as well. It all starts from and returns to you. In the 'Who Do You Work For' circle, the arrows go in all directions. You work for you, so you can take care of others, so they can take care of the customer. When everyone feels taken care of in this circle, everyone wins, and the company is in a better place to achieve profitability.

This works in the best possible way when every employee works from a place where they are taking care of themselves, as well as everybody else. Employees do not like to be used and will often retaliate against employers who use them. This retaliation can take place in many areas and is best to avoid at all costs. How? By not being the type of employer who uses their employees without offering adequate rewards.

The caveat here is that it is up to the employee to learn that the world is not actually all about them. It is up to them to learn how to create offers – i.e.., 'What can I do for you?' – for an employer or potential employer. Most companies do not care about a potential employee. Companies care about themselves and what a potential employee can offer to help the company solve their problems. Employees must create offers inside a company and provide real value. Otherwise, they are just another cog in the wheel. Through their language and their actions, an employee must prove that the company is more valuable with them as an employee. The employers' job is to create a space for that to happen.

When an employer creates a space for employees to rise and helps them to learn how to make valuable offers, everyone in the company benefits; it is a symbiotic relationship.

Honesty and Integrity

"Waste no more time arguing about what a good man should be. Be one." - *Marcus Aurelius*

It is important for managers to always communicate in a way that conveys truthfulness, fairness, and straightforwardness. It is through these that honesty and trust appear and are maintained. Further, it is by these that integrity is earned. Integrity is an assessment that others make about us that has three facets: 1) we act consistently with requests and promises, always producing the conditions of fulfillment by the specified time; 2) we speak and act consistently with our public declarations; and 3) we speak and act consistently with already existing or historical standards of integrity in the community.

It is important for managers to act in a way that builds trust with employees and earns their assessment of our overall integrity. Managers, in turn, extend trust to all employees. This acts to produce an environment that creates trustworthy employees. If a manager cannot build mutual trust and be trusted or assessed with integrity by their employees, they have failed as a manager. All the rest of their actions in the management domain will be meaningless and ineffectual.

Being trustworthy IS all it is cracked up to be.

Creating Trust

"The best way to find out if you can trust somebody is to trust them."
- Ernest Hemingway

Whole books have been written about Trust. It is an area that you can explore in many ways with many people. Trust is not always what we think it is. For example, if there is someone whom you do not Trust because they are always giving away secrets, then they are someone you can Trust to do exactly that. There may be a time and a situation that calls for you to Trust that person to do what they always do. It may be the fastest way to spread the information you wish to spread.

A leader's job is to create Trust and to create a place where Trust is a shared experience. If an employer does not Trust their staff, then the staff usually does not Trust the employer. I find that the opposite is also true, and this truth creates a more hospitable work environment.

A leader creates Trust by being trustworthy themselves and then extending Trust to others. By embodying and extending Trust, a leader automatically creates a trustful environment. A leader also creates Trust by making and keeping promises, just like we ask the employees to do.

According to Paul J. Zak, the founding director of the Center for Neuroeconomics Studies and the author of *Trust Factor: The Science of Creating High-Performance Companies*, when you compare people at low-trust companies to people at high-trust companies, the high-trust employees experience 74% less stress, 106% more energy at work, 50% higher productivity, 13% fewer sick days, 76% more engagement, 29% more satisfaction with their lives, 40% less burnout. They felt a greater sense of accomplishment, as well—41% more. It appears obvious that building and creating trust is vital for any business.

At our restaurants, we specify what our promises are allowing the employees to 'see' that we are making and fulfilling promises recurrently. They will be able to make the assessment that we, as employers, are trustworthy. We make these promises in the Employee Handbook as well as at company meetings and in one-on-one meetings. Some of the basic promises we make are listed below:

> Payday is Wednesday by 2:00 pm.
> The paycheck will not bounce.
> A fair wage will be paid.
> The work schedule for the following week is posted by 5:00 pm on Wednesday.
> The schedule will be fair and balanced.
> We will fix any broken equipment.
> We will hire effective people.
> We will get rid of ineffective people.
> We will create a safe and fun work environment.
> The business finances and metrics are available to all who want to see them.

By making and keeping the above promises, we create an environment of Trust. By extending Trust to employees and following up with them in those trusted positions, we are creating an environment of Trust.

Other ways of building Trust include recognizing excellence, communicating clear and attainable goals, allowing people leeway in how they work (by not micromanaging), continually educating and training employees, encouraging upward growth, showing concern for the whole employee (not just the work employee), and allowing them space to do their jobs. As Paul J. Zack goes on to say: "Ultimately, you cultivate trust by setting a clear direction, giving people what they need to see it through, and getting out of their way."

Just like the Hemingway quotation says above, the best way to find out if you can Trust someone is to put them in a position of Trust. If the right environment has been created, you will find that most people are trustworthy.

Using the diagram below, we can see exactly where Trust can be broken in the simple act of making a request. It may be difficult to follow as it is not fully intuitive, so here is the synopsis: 1. Do not make requests and then withdraw them suddenly. 2. Do not make requests and withdraw them after someone has promised to fulfill on your request, this shows a lack of Trust and concern for the employee. 3. Never withdraw a request after the promisor has completed the requested task – that makes you a jerk. If you are good with diagrams and want to know more, continue below, or you can just go to the next chapter.

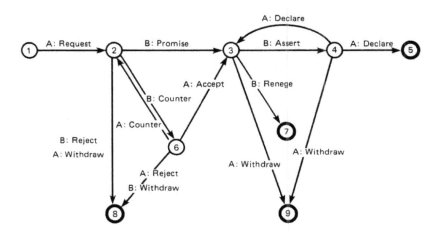

Figure 8 – The Basic Conversation for Action

You can see each location where the requester (A:) withdraws their request in the diagram below. From 2 to 8, the requester has withdrawn the request just after making it. While this is not inherently ineffective in building Trust, it does send a message to the promisor that perhaps they are not up to the task. Do that too often to a person, and you are not building Trust.

From 3 to 9, the request has been withdrawn after the promisor indicated that they can complete the task. You do not want to do this to the same person too often, or they will begin to believe that you do not Trust them.

From 4 to 9, you can see that the request has been withdrawn after the promisor declares that they have fulfilled the request. Nothing lets someone know you do not value them than by engaging in this type of behavior. This type of behavior creates an environment of mistrust and shows just how ineffectual and untrustworthy the requester is in this transaction and possibly many others. This last one will have employees making the assessment that the requester is a jerk, and nobody likes working for a jerk.

Moods and Managing Mood

"Do you have moods? Or do your moods have you?"
- Barry Jessurun

When I was in my twenties and bartending at a fast-paced nightclub as a second job, I would often come in and be thrown into a bad mood because the opening bartenders did not do an adequate job of setting up the bar for a successful night. I would have to begin my shift, not by making drinks and taking care of customer service, but by having to set up my station and, often-times, backing up the other stations so that we could have a successful night. I often did this in a bad mood that I blamed on the other bartenders and the manager, who did not do anything about it even after I brought it to her attention. Once I got busy making drinks, my mood changed, and I was able to have fun. At that time, I had no idea that my bad mood was my own fault and that I was the only one who could fix the problem. Many years later, I was able to learn how to manage my expectations and manage my own mood in most situations.

Truthfully, it was not until I was in my thirties that I was able to become more effective in managing my mood. When we first opened The Vanilla Bean Café, I found I was often in a bad mood when I felt that I was doing most of the work and my family partners were not functioning the way that I thought they should. They were not living up to my expectations. When I was able to settle into the job and adjust my expectations and job descriptions, I was in a much better place to manage my moods. I realized that it was my expectations, along with no real job descriptions, that was causing me to blame the others for my bad moods. I was trying to use my bad mood to communicate my displeasure to people who did not understand my displeasure. I wanted them to change because I was in a bad mood, which I thought they caused. That is kind of like taking a poison and hoping the other person gets sick. Open communication and clear expectations helped me to become more effective. It did not happen overnight. For many years, I was one of those jerks who acted out of their bad mood and would cause people around me to suffer. I am glad I got over that.

The question here is, are your moods disproportionate to a given situation? You may be experiencing uncomfortable emotions due to the inability to manage your moods. The many challenges of today's culture seem to provoke mood swings for many people, which can cause damage to relationships, careers, and even affect a person's physical health. You may be unaware that you can control these moods (through mindfulness, practice, and time). If you choose to explore this possibility and work to strengthen your control, you can change outcomes in your daily life and work.

One of my teachers always said that, "Mood is 90% of everything." It is the positive mood that we all want to live with and work with. We all live in moods. Advertisers work to create moods. Businesses generate moods. We buy, sell, and live in and with moods throughout our life. Learning how to recognize your own moods, how to generate moods, and how to manage moods within yourself and in others is an integral part of leadership and in living a good and mindful lives. This ability to manage mood allows you to take care of yourself and what you care about and to create a space in which you and those around you can flourish. I imagine that the remaining 10% of everything is the underlying 'stuff' we call life, but I am just guessing here, as he never told us.

Moods are generated by thoughts and feelings that arise inside your body based on external triggers, your own history, the story you have for your future self, and how that all manifests in the present moment. These moods are often generated by ungrounded assessments of the present situation and your internal dialogue. Thoughts and feelings triggered in a specific situation are not necessarily the truth and should never be regarded as such. They are there to help guide us in creating a more effective action in the moment and generate a better future for ourselves and those we care about. To create your own mood, you need to be mindful of your present situation, know what you care about, and take actions that take care of those concerns. This is called your narrative or your long-term story of care. It is something that you should always be working on and creating.

Designing, building, and creating your narrative is an important first step in managing your mood. When practiced, this ability, coupled with mindfulness, will lead you to understand how to manage your mood, and trigger moods in others, as well as effectively manage the mood of the workplace. To be a more effective leader, it is crucial to knowing what you care about and identify the most effective course of action for addressing those concerns in the present moment. Essentially, your job is to be a storyteller: first, as the teller of your own story, and then as the teller of the company story in a way that includes others and resonates for them and the futures they are working to create for themselves. Your job as storyteller is to create and maintain an environment in which you are happy and can effectively take care of yourself and others. Being able to do this on a recurrent basis will generate a mood in which people will want to be engaged. Your main concern as a leader should be to create a place where others want to be. They will want to be there because your business is a place that takes care of their immediate concerns and helps them with their own long-term story of what they care about (their own narrative).

When you experience moods you do not want, first know that they are not the absolute truth. They are triggered within you by an assessment based on the current situation, your own story about the immediate present moment, your short-term outlook, and your long-term narrative. Often it is unmet expectations that cause a negative mood. That is why you will often hear people talking about managing expectations. It is important to have clear and attainable expectations, knowing that things will always find a way of going wrong. Be prepared for breakdowns. This preparation should be built into your expectations. Expectations are part of your personal narrative and relatively easy to locate within your awareness and the first step toward control and change. If you believe that everything will always go according to plan and get upset because it does not, you need to reevaluate your expectations and change the narrative.

Do not blame other people. When you expect things to go wrong, you start to plan for breakdowns automatically and will be able to handle them effectively in a good mood. It comes down to this: change your thoughts (narrative), and you will subsequently change how you respond to life's situations. Know that this takes time and practice.

Managers who act out of negative moods based on ungrounded assessments will undermine their own authority and betray their future concerns. In their leadership position, they will derail the entire work environment. People who consistently act out of ineffective or negative moods are destructive to the work environment and will essentially lose their team's respect. They are selfishly saying, "Fuck everyone, I am in a bad mood." Not only is this self-destructive, but it is also detrimental to building relationships, developing trust, and creating an effective team. No one I know wants to work with or especially around someone like that and certainly will not do so for long.

Acting out of your negative moods can be viewed as a form of bullying. When acting out of your bad mood, you are telling your team and those around you that your commitment to your bad mood is more important than they are and that they will just have to deal with it. This form of self-indulgence is narcissistic, and it blinds you to what you really need to be taking care of in the present moment. In business, this care should always be directed toward the staff, the customer, and the long-term viability of the business. True, taking care of yourself with mindful and healthful practices should always come first, but never in a way that betrays your team, your business, or your customers.

To change your mood or the mood of the workplace, you must be aware of your own moods and what the trigger points are. You need to be mindful of them and then choose how to act to create effective outcomes in every given situation. You must first identify the moods you are experiencing, along with what may be causing them to manifest. By being mindful, and present with your thoughts, you can be aware of negative thought patterns. To begin the process, you may want to take inventory of what currently is not working for you in your job or in your life. Troubling relationships, health concerns, or financial struggles could be contributing to your unmanaged moods. Only when you have done the work to manage your moods will you be able to manage the mood of the workplace.

When people ask me what it is I do for work each day, I tell them I am a storyteller who uses language to manage mood and invent reality. If I had put that statement at the beginning of this book, you might have thought I was a little crazy. Which, who knows, I may be. What do you think?

What do I mean when I say I manage mood and invent reality? I start by managing my mood and work to make sure that I am in a good and well-grounded mood before I engage my workplace and my employees. I then make an effort to engage in such a way that can generate the mood of the employees and the workplace. I might check in with each employee, ask how they are doing, tell a joke, point out how well they are doing, etc., anything that will have a positive effect on the overall mood of each individual and the place as a whole. As far as inventing reality goes, I am the principal storyteller. I language the business into existence. I work each day with my language, my words, my story to create and co-create with the employees, customers, and vendors the place in which we all interact. I take responsibility for this. I do not just let it happen. Something is going to happen; I just work in such a way that happens in line with the way I would like it to come into existence. Without me, the reality of our business would not exist. And I want it to exist with an overall mood of fun.

Another major trigger that can affect your mood is taking something personally that someone says or does. You are tempted to respond as if it were being done to you without thinking at all about the situation, the people involved, who is making the statement, or about your self-worth. When something upsets you or makes you feel uncomfortable, it is helpful to logically assess the situation. Does the situation call for the reaction you are experiencing, or are you 'losing it' unnecessarily? Is the other person really doing something wrong or to you, or are you taking the situation too personally? Is their mood a reflection of your actions? Could you do something to check your deteriorating mood?

"Do not take anything personally, nothing others do is because of you. What others say and do is a projection of their own reality, their own dream [story/narrative]. When you are immune to the opinions and actions of others, you won't be the victim of needless suffering."
- Miguel Ruiz - The Four Agreements.

If you do not consciously acknowledge the unmet expectations triggering your emotional reactions, you will feel imprisoned by your own emotions. On the other hand, if you honestly look at yourself and see the expectations you cling to, you can begin to view life more objectively. You will free yourself up to choose your responses to people in the future, start taking more responsibility for yourself and remain more emotionally neutral, hence managing your mood.

Training **and** Education

"Tell me and I forget, teach me and I may remember, involve me and I learn." - Benjamin Franklin

We like to use the word education along with the word training as we work with all employees. Training is just showing how a task is completed, while education goes beyond the work and gives the reason(s) for why we do what we do. An employee must know what the restaurant does on all levels, why we do what we do, and what our mission and goals are to be able to function as an effective employee.

There are three phases in the learning process: familiarity, understanding, and knowledge. We will use the game of golf as an example to help us understand the difference. Familiarity is just that – someone has heard of golf but does not know anything about it, other than it is played outside, and you use clubs to hit a ball into a hole. Understanding golf means that you have learned all about the game; you know about the different clubs that can be used, you know about the ball and why it is dimpled, you know about the greens and sand traps, you understand the par system and how to score the game. Since you have watched the pros on TV, you have seen it played well. With all this understanding, it could be possible that you have never played the game or that you are a beginner player. Understanding is what is taught in most schools today and does not fully prepare you for the world of work. Knowledge is the embodiment of all that is required to fulfill a task effectively and recurrently; you can play golf well. While you still may need coaching because you are always working to get better, you can function well and educate and train others effectively. Knowledge is obtained only by 'doing' something recurrently with your body. The pro-golfer is a good example of this.

When you work with employees, always try to do so in a way that not only trains them but also educates them about all the jobs that they will learn while employed as well. As a manager, work to engage your staff so that they can become knowledgeable of the work that they perform (embodied knowledge). Work patiently with them through the learning process, as this always takes time, and it will be different for each employee. Involve them in the practice of the job, tell them why a certain thing is done a certain way. Help to build in them a deeper understanding of the task or job at hand; by doing so, you will help them grow. Through their continued practice toward having the embodied knowledge that characterizes a well-rounded employee, a person will develop into one who understands the 'why' as well as the 'how' of the job. With time, employees who have this degree of education may be able to find a more effective way of completing the job. They may find a better and cost-saving approach to the job. I have seen this repeatedly with our employees, whom we have not only trained but educated.

Motivate or Mobilize?

"If I have to motivate you, it means I have to get rid of you."
- Barry Jessurun

People often think that it is the manager's job to motivate employees. If you have read this far, you have probably learned that this is not what we want our managers to do. It is the human resource person's job to bring in the right people who seem able to self-motivate; it is the manager's job to create an environment where this is possible and encouraged. The story of any work environment should be a compelling one in which the employee wants to take part. It is the manager's job to keep that story alive by always speaking about the quality of our overall offer and why we are here. It is also important for employees to hear how their effective work with us will greatly impact their future worth to new employers and on anything they choose to do in their lives. It is this conversation that can help mobilize an employee and boost their motivation. *They* are here because *they* want to be here. *They* are here because *they* can connect this work to what *they* will be doing in the future. *They* can see their future value. It is up to the manager to engage the employees in conversations that convey and reinforce this vision.

An employee must have a future story that resonates for them and builds assurance that working in the moment will help them to be more valuable in that future they are working to create. Without this story, it is impossible to mobilize an employee. Mobilization happens from within; it is not based on external input. It will be shaped by external input. It will be challenged by the environment in which they function, but the onus of responsibility for being mobilized and motivated rests solely upon each employee. The manager's job is to be the positive trigger in their environment that mobilizes them, not to be there all the time to motivate them.

An interview is a conversation where both parties are exploring who the other person is and if there could be a mutually beneficial future together. It is not unlike dating. Once, when I was interviewing someone for a manager position, the interviewee posed an interesting question to me. During the second interview with this person, I was asked what I would do to motivate employees. If I remember correctly, my first response was to laugh. Then I calmly informed this person that it is not my job to motivate employees; it is not my job to motivate anyone, except myself. Further, I told this candidate that, as a manager, they would be required to carry out the manager's duties without any expectations that I, as the owner, would motivate them. I said that if they personally find the job challenging and rewarding for learning and growth, then the job will be the motivating factor. People choose to work with us because it also works for them. While we do offer profit sharing for key managers, it is not tied to achieving any concrete goals. Work, have Fun, create value, make, and fulfill requests effectively, foster a positive and hospitable environment, generate profit: that is basically the job. We do not motivate the employee. I suggested that the candidate think about our stance and call us back if there was still interest in the job. I never received a call. It obviously did not work for this person to function as a manager in an environment where they expected to be self-mobilized. Our job is to create a place where the right person shows up or self-selects to be there. This place we create with our stories helps the candidate to self-mobilize because it works for their current story about their life.

Motivation can be intrinsic or extrinsic. Intrinsic or internal motivation is what I call mobilization. It is a story about yourself that motivates you into action. Extrinsic or external stimuli that motivate you into action I call manipulation. Manipulation does not always carry the negative connotation that our culture implies. There are many people who make a living by manipulating others into action. As long as each party is a willing participant in the transaction, there is not a problem. The problem arises when someone is willfully and secretively manipulating another as a means to someone's own end. I encourage you to develop your intrinsic motivation, your own story, to motivate you into action. It is fine to rely on external motivation, but you will create a more effective self when you can self-motivate in the long run.

Now, what about you? Do you need to be motivated? Or does your own story about your life mobilize you into effective action? Suppose you believe that you need to be motivated by your employer or anyone else for that matter. In that case, you need to begin a conversation about your own ambitions and what you believe about the future toward which you are headed. You and your story about the future are all you have; no one is going to do it for you. You are either the main character in your own life story, and it is a compelling story that motivates you into effective action, or you are a minor character in many other stories.

Your story needs to mobilize you into effective action that helps to create a more valuable you. Your story should not need a supporting cast to motivate you into action. It does, however, need a supporting cast. To do just that, support.

If you believe that your job is to mobilize others, what you really need to work on is a compelling story that foresees the right people showing up who want to work with you. You need to create a positive and hospitable environment that is mutually beneficial. You need to function to create a mood of inclusion and growth. It is the story that attracts and mobilizes the right people into action. Working to motivate people is a waste of time. If a person feels they need to be motivated, then they need help in creating a new or better story so it fits with where they are in the moment, or they need to find another place that fits their old story.

I have found that the process of continually improving my story – what I do I do for myself and the future I am working to create – mobilizes me into action, no matter where or with whom I find myself working. I have worked some jobs that sucked, but I always gave them my best effort. Why? Because I was doing it for myself. I learned a lot of varied and valuable things along the way, and I found that I could work with and around a variety of different employers. I developed many skills and created a much more valuable me. It is our job to motivate and mobilize ourselves. If not, why bother at all?

Familiarity, Understanding, and Knowledge

"Learning is not attained by chance; it must be sought for with ardor and attended to with diligence." - Abigail Adams

I am about to repeat myself from the Training and Education chapter, and I have deliberately created a chapter on this as well; I just use a different sport this time. Think of it as reading about it again for the first time.

Learning has three distinct phases: familiarity, understanding, and knowledge. This can best be seen in sports, so let us use tennis as an example. Most people in the U.S. are familiar with the sport of tennis; this means that they know that it is played on a court, you use rackets and a ball, and they may know that the ball is usually yellow and fuzzy. When someone has an understanding of tennis, they know the rules, the different kinds of courts that tennis can be played on, how the score is kept, the different kinds of strokes there are, along with the different styles of play. They can know all there is to know about tennis, including its history. They could pass a written test about tennis, and at the same time, they do not even ever have to play the game. This is understanding. This is what most schools teach. The subsequent effect of this is that many people often confuse understanding with knowledge. Knowledge is what you can DO recurrently with your body. Professional tennis players are paid for their knowledge, not for what they understand about tennis. This is true in all professions; it is just not as visible in other professions. There, repetition over.

I find it extremely important to have these distinctions when working with young people because they will often confuse understanding with knowledge. When they engage in that type of language and thinking, they shut down potential learning. Of course, I see this with older employees as well, who come from a place of certainty where they think they know something when all they have is understanding. Learning how to communicate with employees and expose them to something new can be very challenging at times because they think they already know something. At the same time, I must be careful not to fall into the trap of thinking I know something, where I can also shut down learning something from my employees. I do learn things from my employees, but I have to be mindful and not always behave and think in such a way that I am not open to new learning.

I enjoy working with younger people because they are more malleable, they are more open to learning and they tend to be more eager to learn something new. It comes naturally to them. They intuitively know that they are in the understanding phase and that it is knowledge that they seek. They also do not fall into the trap of certainty very quickly. They do not like to hear 'that is the way things are done' and are more open to question our practices. It is because of this that I learn new things from my staff. It is because of this, that we are always listening to them for new and more effective ways to accomplish something. Older employees will also innovate, but they tend to bring something with them from other places and do not see the situation as a 'new' one. Just because something worked well in one place does not mean it will translate in another. Adapting existing understanding to a new situation to come up with something new is innovation, and while we all do this, I find younger people do it more often. In the hospitality industry, we tend to say that older employees, while they bring with them knowledge, they also bring with them bad habits. And habits are difficult to change and can be difficult to manage.

This idea that understanding = knowledge causes a lot of problems in the workplace. Businesses rely on the consistency of their product and/or service to attract and retain customers and hence produce income (and hopefully a profit – more on that later). I often encounter employees who cut corners and compromise the integrity of the offer. When they are questioned about their actions and re-told the right (effective) way to accomplish the task, I am told by them, "I know." I tell them that if they knew, I would not be talking with them. What they have is understanding. If they do not do it recurrently without cutting corners, they do not "know" how to do the task. Doing something effectively and repeatedly is knowledge, and knowledge is something for which employers are willing to pay more.

An example I use at the Bean is how a sandwich is made. There are many ways to make a sandwich and many ways to layer the ingredients. There is no one 'right way.' Someone will work for me who has worked as a sandwich maker somewhere else and inform me that we do not make sandwiches the 'right way.' At the Bean, there is only one way: the Bean's way. It is not the 'right way,' it is not the 'wrong way', it is our way. Done consistently, it is the effective way. Consistency is why customers return. So, I will find an employee making a sandwich in a way other than the Bean's way and correct them. They inform me that they 'know' how to make a sandwich. Guess what I say? Right, "If you 'knew,' I wouldn't be talking to you." What they have is their own understanding about how to make a sandwich, when they know our way and can do it the same way all the time then they will know how to make a sandwich for customers at the Bean. The restaurant business is all about consistency, when a customer gets a menu item and enjoys that item, they want it the same way the next time they visit. Employees get paid for their knowledge of this and their ability to fulfill on our offer consistently over time.

So, what do you 'know' that you only understand, and what are you going to do about it? How do you become knowledgeable when you only have understanding? The first step is to be aware that you only have understanding. The second step is to be open to learning, or as we say at our restaurants, be in a mood of willingness. Then, of course, practice, practice, practice. Ask any professional athlete. Get the best coach, be open to learning and improving constantly, and continually practice with a goal of improvement.

More importantly, how are you going to engage with others to help them be more open to learning?

Thinking and believing something to be true and 'right' gets in the way of learning something new or deepening your current understanding. Watch your own thinking and be aware when you are getting in your own way. Always work to attain workable knowledge. It is what professionals get paid for.

This way of looking at learning is only my interpretation. There are many ways of looking at how we learn that can be equally effective. I find that breaking it down into these three phases helps everyone 'see' the aspects of learning. They can then work to learn in an effective manner, which leads to attaining knowledge, that creates value in their future. It also helps each of us track our progress as we journey together through the learning process.

Most importantly, it shows that it is knowledge for which professionals get paid.

Standard Practices

Every day you should have a plan. It does not mean that you must stick to the plan entirely every day, but you need to have a plan. Each day of the week might have a different plan. It may change every week. Still, have a plan. That being said, as part of your planning, you should enumerate those jobs that need to be completed on particular days. This is called having a standard practice, where these parts of the business must be accomplished on the same day each week, by the same time each month, by the same time each year. By having standard practices that you engage in each day, each week, and so on, you develop habits that become ingrained. By creating these standard practices, you create balance in your workday; you create balance in your life.

In our business, we write checks on Monday. Payroll is delivered to each restaurant by 2:00 pm every Wednesday. Weekly management reports are available every Tuesday by noon. We go to the bank every Monday and Friday. Even if the Monday is a holiday, the deposit is made via the night deposit box. We post the schedule by 4:00 pm every Thursday. We do all ordering on the same days of the week. We have so many standard practices; the days go relatively smoothly. Not only that, but it is also easy to educate a new employee into our standard practices because they are just that: standard practices.

Sure, things go wrong. We may not always keep our promises (which is what they are). We can be affected by numerous things daily: power outages, the internet going down, deliveries at the wrong time, employees who call out sick. These breakdowns and many more happen all the time. We expect these problems to happen, and we have built in other practices to take care of the breakdowns. Because we anticipate problems and always plan for them, we often find we have already made a backup plan to help us keep our promise when a problem arises.

The main thing is not to let daily breakdowns stop you from developing or sticking to your standard practices. The more you engage in working with standard practices, the more they become 'ready-at-hand,' easily done without much planning or forethought. When you achieve this level of organization, you will be able to dedicate more time to working on other important daily or weekly demands of the job.

This is Where You Work

"You are a product of your environment. So, choose the environment that will best develop you toward your objective. Analyze your life in terms of its environment. Are the things around you helping you toward success - or are they holding you back?" - W. Clement Stone

When we opened our second restaurant, one of the (many) things I told our managing partner was to create a place you want to work every day. Spend time, energy, and resources in creating the best possible environment that brings you joy just going to work. Otherwise, why else are you even doing this? Your best possible environment includes the physical space, the overall offer, and the employees with whom you will engage every day. We all play minor roles in creating this kind of space where we work.

In many of the jobs that I have had, I would make changes that created the kind of place I wanted to show up to every day. While I could not change everything I wanted, I could make small changes that made a difference and reduced the difficulty I encountered.

One place where I worked in Boston required one shift to arrive at 9:00 am. This proved to be difficult for almost everyone responsible for that shift because of the craziness of Boston's rush hour. I proposed changing the schedule so that this shift would show up at 10:00 am instead. It was a simple change, but it helped the overall mood of everyone who arrived at that time, which helped the overall mood of the place.

At another job where I was responsible for hiring, I always made an effort to hire people I truly liked. I would sometimes pass up a more qualified candidate because I felt that they would not be a good fit for the culture that I was working to create. Sometimes I hired someone that turned out to be a bad fit. I would work with them to see if they would 'step up' and make the necessary changes to be an integral part of the team. If they could, that was great. If they could not or did not want to, I would teach them the skill of quitting. For some reason, in our culture, we are never encouraged to quit something that is not working for us. We are told to 'stick it out,' 'it will get better,' or 'do not be a quitter.' I have found that helping someone to quit a job that they believe they are not suited for is an important thing to do. I tell our managers who are responsible for the hiring of staff that they will know they have done a good job when someone they helped quit, or even had to fire, comes back to them and says thank you.

That brings me back to the managing partner at our second restaurant. I encouraged him to create a team of people he wanted to see every day. If he came into work and saw an employee and groaned or sought to avoid them, it was important to take note of it and either work to engage this employee or remove them from the staff. The chances are that if you are having trouble with an employee, most likely everyone else is also. By removing people who do not fit the culture, you are helping every other employee in the place. This was a hard lesson for me to learn.

I would often work too hard and spend too much time with an employee who never even asked for help. I was sabotaging the entire staff while I worked to help this one employee who was not a good fit. By working so hard to help them to become a better employee for me and their fellow workers, I would often be doing a disservice to the rest of the staff, as I put up with the many breakdowns precipitated by that one employee. After many years of creating this suffering for myself, I was able to realize that I was not really helping anyone; I was helping because I wanted to and, perhaps, felt I needed to be the helper. I was finally able to see the problems I was causing the rest of the staff. While we still err on the side of helping our staff become better versions of themselves, we have a line that we no longer cross and find that removing them from the team benefits both them and the team.

It is up to the management to create a place where everyone, from the employees to the customers, wants to be. If there are employees who do not fit the mold, it is crucial to either help them to rise or help them to leave and move on. This also holds true for our customers. If there are difficult customers who derail the entire staff, it may be a good time to tell them not to come back. This may be an unknown fact, but difficult customers are costly. In my experience, I have seen employees quit jobs because the owner or manager refused to get rid of an abusive customer. When an employer sides with the customer in a difficult situation, the staff takes notice. The employer's first customers should always be the staff, so if the owner or manager does not prioritize the staff over a difficult customer, then the good staff will leave to find an employer who values them.

Everything comes back to creating an environment you want to work in every day, with employees and customers that bring a smile to your face and joy to your heart. If you work there, then you are responsible for creating the environment. Here is a rule you can test for yourself: if your workplace is a place where you want to work every day, then it is most likely a place where other people will want to spend time as well, be they employees or customers. Take this responsibility to heart and create to the best of your ability. You are the artist. Make it so.

Cash Flow

"Entrepreneurs believe that profit is what matters most in a new enterprise. But profit is secondary. Cash flow matters most." - Peter Drucker

Do you have $20 in your pocket right now? Congratulations, you have positive cash flow! In business and in personal finances, it is all about cash flow. Money in, money out, money saved – income, expense, profit. Household income is fairly easy to predict, business income not so much. Businesses are at the mercy of the weather, the seasons, and a myriad of other events that come and go throughout the year. Predicting business income can be difficult, but I have learned that the law of averages works in our favor. Profit (your savings goal) shows up mostly through controlling expenses. In the food business, the two most controllable expenses are the money spent on food purchases and the money spent on labor. While saving money by switching phone providers could save you money in your household budget, it is almost meaningless in the budget of a busy restaurant. That does not stop us from working to get the best rates from our electric and telephone companies, since small changes do add up to larger amounts over the period of a year.

The best way to create a positive cash flow in your household finances and hence some savings is to create a budget. These days you can find budgeting tools in a lot of places. There are online services, hard copy spread sheets, and personal finance programs like Quicken, to name a few. Simply by budgeting your monthly income and expenses, you can come up with ways to cut some expenses and create a savings plan.

When you oversee the purchasing for a busy restaurant, you learn a lot about budgeting and cash flow. We create a budget on Monday in our restaurants and then revisit it again on Thursday after looking at current expenses and the long-term weather forecast. We adjust the budget up or down based on those factors. The budget on

148

Monday is based on four years of previous business, the weather forecast, and any events that may be happening that will influence our amount of business. We also create a yearly budget for capital expenses and a very informal five-year plan for long-term liabilities. All this factors into our overall monthly review of income, expenses, and overall product cost.

We adjust on a daily, weekly, and monthly basis, and in the five-year plan, we consider the monthly expense of all long-term loan payments – just as you might do when you want to purchase a new car or make some other big household expense.

Simply put, creating a budget and learning how to create positive cash flow will go a long way in helping you to reach your own long-term financial goals. If you do not keep track and measure it, you will not have the knowledge you need to make the necessary changes to create the savings plan that you want.

Before I oversaw ordering at a restaurant, I had a good grasp of budgeting. Because of what I learned while working, I was able to manage our household finances much more effectively. I hear a lot of people say that they do not have time or that they are not good with numbers. The problem here is that they are being self-limiting and creating their own less-than-ideal reality. Things would improve markedly for them if they changed their conversations to something like this, "While I have not been good with numbers in the past, I am now working on a household budget and determined to get better at it."

I could go on about the importance of understanding the numbers while operating a business. I have become quite good at it. But I will not take you down that road. Just know that the numbers picture will begin to improve by beginning to give the numbers your attention. If you do not measure, you will not know if you are improving. A budget helps you measure. Professional sports and athletes are great at this. If there is any one business where people keep impeccable records and stats, it is professional sports. That is why they are Professional Sports. They measure, and they seek to improve.

A budget, whether household or business, allows you to keep your own statistics, and this can be a tool to help you improve.

Sticking with the title, it is all about managing cash flow. Many people think that all they need to do is make more money, and the cash flow problem will be solved. That is not always true in business and not always true in personal finances. In the words of Robert Kiyosaki (American businessman, author, and founder of Rich Global LLC and the Rich Dad Company): "Making more money will not solve your problems if cash flow management is your problem."

Learn to Budget

"Budgeting is not just for people who do not have enough money.
It is for everyone who wants to ensure that their money is enough."
- Rosette Mugidde Wamambe

I first learned about budgeting from my parents and then in a home economics class in high school. My understanding of the budgeting process helped me navigate my first year living in Boston in my late teens. Going to school, working, and earning enough money to pay rent and food was a close call every month. Understanding cash flow and the use of a budget, all while being debt averse, helped me immensely. I remember when I had to first carry a balance on my credit card, I almost cried. I had to replace two tires on my car at one time, and it set me back. I did not like the feeling. From that point on, I have worked not to carry a balance on my credit card.

There are all kinds of tools available to help someone new to budgeting understand the process. There are free spreadsheet templates and budgeting tools in programs like Quicken that also help. In my teens, it did not take much. I had a certain income and predictable expenses. I used a budget on and off throughout my twenties, based on my income, but because I was a bartender, I used my check to cover my monthly expenses and my tips for play money.

Owning a restaurant helped me to understand budgeting on a whole new level. It is one thing to create a budget based on your known income, but in almost any business, the income is always a projection. I had to decide on how much money we could spend based on the money I thought we were going to have. Sometimes I was right, sometimes I was wrong. Because it is all based on weekly and monthly cash flows, I always had the ability to correct overspending and underspending each week. There are many times we order based on the long-term weather forecast because our business is greatly affected by the weather. I would put in a big order based on a great weekend weather report, and then it would change, which would reduce the number of customers and would result in a larger inventory and overspending on our initial budget.

In the restaurant business, we base our budgets on our business metrics. Every business has its own metrics based on where the business is located, what business they are in, who their customer is, the cost of the product or service, and what the customer spends. The cost of the product or service is known as Costs of Goods Sold or COGS. In the restaurant, we refer to the cost of food, the cost of any packaging for the food, and the cost of the labor to produce the food as the prime cost. We budget for the labor cost and the food cost every week. All the other costs of business are referred to as fixed costs and do not usually vary much or are adjusted based on the time of the year. For example, electricity in the summer months will cost more because of the cost of running the air conditioning. The cost of gas will be higher in the winter months due to the cost of heating. These costs are generally averaged for the whole year and budgeted evenly throughout the year if cash flow is strong.

Learning all of this helped me run our household budget in a more detailed way that helped us to run the household expenses in a more effective way. We set savings goals, investment goals, and education goals, along with play or vacation goals. Some years were easy; some years were difficult. That is the way it is when you run a business that does not have a regular income each year. If I had a job that paid me the same amount each year, it would have been easier.

Learning how to budget your money is not a hard thing to do. Practicing the process each month will be helpful to your long-term financial goals (i.e., buying a house, saving for a vacation, saving for education, etc.). A simple internet search will help you find an easy-to-use spreadsheet for this practice. If you currently carry any debt, it is important to know that having too much debt is not a debt problem; it is a budgeting problem. Using a budget will help you to understand cash flow and will guide you in a way to make decisions that keep you from living beyond your means.

From the song *The Low Spark of High Heeled Boys* by Stevie Winwood and Jim Capaldi:

> *The percentage you're paying is too high a price*
> *While you're living beyond all your means*
> *And the man in the suit has just bought a new car*
> *From the profit he's made on your dreams*

When you carry debt from buying things you do not need or cannot afford, the rich get richer.

Back-timing

"By failing to prepare, you are preparing to fail."
- Benjamin Franklin

I am sure you have heard about time management. As we go through our schooling, we are told to budget our time wisely and develop good time management skills. This allows for us to keep many of our other promises that rely on being on time. "Back-timing" is a way to develop good skills in this area.

Back-timing is a time management term that comes from radio and television broadcasting. It is a technique used to make sure all the stories fit into the show, and you can transition to the next show on time. A manager assigns a time estimate to each story depending on how important it is. All those time estimates add up to fill the newscast. All the news of the day, sports, weather, and entertainment need to fit in that timespan.

We all do this throughout our day without even realizing that we are engaging in back-timing. When we have to drive somewhere and arrive at a specific time, we add to the minimum drive time (no stops) however much extra time it will take for any elective stops we wish to make along the way. Since the time of day can influence drive time, we must, during a "rush hour," factor in possible or likely delays. Only after all that factoring do we decide on what time we need to leave to arrive on time.

Some people excel at this type of deliberate time management. Many do it without realizing what they are doing. Some people just plain suck at this.

In the restaurant industry, back-timing is crucial for meeting the demands of each day, especially if we are going to offer daily specials along with our regular menu. When it comes to catering, it is even more important to be effective in back-timing. I have worked on catering events serving from 10 to 2,000 people, and in each case, the back-timing must be carefully calculated to have the event go as planned. In the case of a 10-person catering gig, it will be relatively simple so that the back-timing can be worked out in a matter of hours. A 2,000-person catering gig will have a back-timing calculation that requires days to complete. In every case, knowing how to plan and how to set up a back-timing schedule will ensure that the event happens on time.

Recently, I began teaching my daughter how to back-time a meal. She did the prep and cooking, but I set up the schedule for when to start each part of the meal so that all aspects of the meal were ready at the same time. She was successful, and now she thinks she knows how to cook.

When I was a kid, I marveled at how my mom could make dinner for eight or more people (six kids, two adults, however many friends), and have it all done simultaneously. Often, she would even have to make something special for a particular child who did not like the night's offering. For example, I have a brother who does not like red sauce. So, when we had spaghetti and meatballs, he would get clam sauce. It amazed me that she could have the entire meal done at the same time. It seemed like magic, and I could not wait to try it myself.

When I was a senior in high school, my parents were away for a week and left me home alone. My older siblings had all moved away, and my younger sister was staying with a friend who could get her to school in the morning. So, what does a high school kid do? I had a party. No, not that kind of party. A dinner party. I was going to back-time a meal for seven of my friends. The menu was roast chicken, rice, vegetables, salad, and bread. I could not wait to get started and went shopping with a level of excitement that surprised me. I did the whole thing: tablecloth, candles, wine, the main meal, and dessert. My back-timing was perfect, and I loved pulling off my first-ever dinner party. Many more were to come. Truth be told, I also invited several other friends to arrive after 9:00 pm for the regular party that kids have when their parents are away.

These days, I use back-timing for all kinds of things throughout my week, from driving to our restaurants to picking up children to going out with friends. I believe that by giving you a word for what you do, almost automatically you will become more adept in developing the skill of back-timing.

Part 3 – Engagement

"The body inherits what the mind engages."
- Brian S. Woods

"Very little is needed to make a happy life;
it is all within yourself, in your way of thinking."
- Marcus Aurelius

Hospitality

"Hospitality is present when something happens for you. It is absent when something happens to you. Those two simple prepositions for and to express it all." - Danny Meyer

Our life, among other things, is about being hospitable to others, creating spaces that encourage repeat visits, whether in our homes, our place of business, or in our hearts. Living every day with an attitude of hospitality toward others helps to create an accepting and peaceful environment. So, embrace the idea of hospitality with everyone you come into daily contact with, be they employees, bosses, vendors, customers, friends, family, etc.

Engage every day with a sense of care and kindness for your fellow humans. It goes a long way.

At our restaurants, we take care of everyone who comes through our door, be it the front door or the back door. It is important for us to take care of our delivery drivers. We make sure that the way is not blocked, that they have easy access to do their jobs. We help them make work easier for everyone. We will often give them beverages: coffee on cold days, cold beverages on hot days, or even a meal occasionally. We treat them as if they were customers. In return, they treat us with care and respect. Drivers have often gone out of their way to make sure that we have the product that we need. There have been times when something was lost on the truck, and when they find it later in the day, they make a return trip to bring it to us. There have been times when the product we ordered was not on the truck, and the drivers have deliberately 'shorted' another customer to make sure we received what we needed. We take care of them; they help to take care of us. This is true in all relationships, but it stems from treating people with care and from a place of hospitality.

The following little snippet by C. E. Murphy, an American-born author based in Ireland, about Irish hospitality vs. American hospitality is very telling:

"In Ireland, you go to someone's house, and she asks you if you want a cup of tea. You say no, thank you, you are really just fine. She asks if you are sure. You say of course you are sure, really, you do not need a thing. Except they pronounce it ting. You do not need a ting. Well, she says then, I was going to get myself some anyway, so it would be no trouble. Ah, you say, well, if you were going to get yourself some, I wouldn't mind a spot of tea, at that, so long as it's no trouble and I can give you a hand in the kitchen. Then you go through the whole thing all over again until you both end up in the kitchen drinking tea and chatting.

In America, someone asks you if you want a cup of tea, you say no, and then you do not get any damned tea.

I liked the Irish way better." - C.E. Murphy

Community

"Alone, we can do so little; together, we can do so much"
- Helen Keller

It is easy to see that a restaurant is a community onto itself, not unlike other work environments where communities are formed by the employees and often with customers. What is not easy to see are the many communities that are touched by a healthy and vibrant restaurant business. Then there are the communities that are created by the existence of a vibrant and healthy restaurant within a community. These are virtually impossible to see.

I have been part of many communities throughout my life, some because of where I was born and grew up. I went to Community School. I was a member of a swim team. Then there were the different communities in my high school; I was part of some of those groups, one of which was my own friend group. Later in my life, I was involved in communities based on my own choices and the workplaces of which I was part. Communities are a natural occurrence for humans and have been necessary for our survival as a species.

While many communities are happenstance, there are also communities of people that have been formed for specific purposes, around different ideologies, with different professional interests, etc. Communities are an integral part of being human, along with our desire to create a better future for some or all involved in them.

The community that forms in a restaurant is happenstance. Different people show up and become employees and form a community. Many restaurants open with the idea of being a community hub where there may not be one in the area. This is one of the main reasons that we opened The Vanilla Bean Café in 1989. There was not one informal place open to the public where all would be welcome and where they could find community. This motivation continued with the opening of our other three restaurants. The one we opened next to The University of Connecticut was intended to be a gathering spot for the Storrs community. It was very heartening to see members of that community begin to meet up at our new Café and tell us how glad they were to have a place where such community was made possible.

Cafés throughout the country and around the world have served many kinds of groups depending on their time and place. It is said that plans for many important historical events have come together in taverns and cafés. Numerous community groups have used our own restaurants for meetings, weddings, parties, educational seminars, artistic gatherings, political events – the list goes on and on. Restaurants that set out to become a hub for communities and live up to their own stories become integral in the everyday lives of the communities they serve. A new restaurant often becomes a catalyst for the vibrancy of its community, and its name and reputation become synonymous with the town in which it operates. When this is created mindfully and with purpose, it creates a space of possibilities that would not have existed without it.

Like with anything, some restaurants create this space exceptionally well, while others are not even aware that community is even a part of the service they can offer.

Our restaurants have always been mindful of the communities they serve and help foster and create. We care for our own internal community and work to make sure it is a safe and harmonious place for our workers. We care about the community at large and make space for different groups to use our space for both public and private events. As a restaurant, we are also part of the community and part of existing communities. We are part of the regional and state restaurant community. We are part of the local business community. We are part of the regional and national entertainment community and have met many great people and formed many friendships over the years. In fact, I met my wife through this community. I was able to be introduced to her because she was part of the music community and was booked for a gig at our establishment. My brother met his wife because she came as an audience member to a show. Speaking of weddings, we know of over 30 couples who met because of the community we help create. I am not saying this because our restaurant is special; I am saying this because it is normal. When people work together and show up together, stuff happens. It is important. Communities are important. Being mindful of communities and fostering their creation is important – which is something restaurants can do well. Restaurants, by nature, are social hubs in the community. By including the community within the business plan, a restaurant will become a vital player in a community's life. This helps the restaurant and, by extension, its employees and other community members to succeed.

The lesson here is not just to provide a hang out at your restaurant. The lesson is to be mindful of the communities in which we live and work and to find ways to help our communities, if possible. All our restaurants contribute to local charitable organizations (communities themselves). At The Vanilla Bean Café, we have been hosting fundraising events since our first year of operation. Organizations we have helped include local food banks, a domestic violence shelter, individual families in need, The Arc, the Connecticut Audubon, and many others. At our other restaurants, we participate in fundraisers for many local organizations. We will often participate in "Tastes," where we donate food and staff for service. We will host guest bartender nights where proceeds go to places like the women's board at the local hospital. We will participate in local golf fundraisers. Again, the list goes on. It is important to note that this work is also all 'Selfishly Altruistic.' We do such events because we want to. They are part of our business plan to engage with the community, and we also do them out of genuine care for others. As we help our community, we expose our offer to a wider network and are included in the marketing that comes with the event. It is a win-win scenario. The bottom line, we love to be an integral part of what is happening in our area.

We also encourage our employees to join community organizations and find ways that they can give back to the community that we call home. For some, it is volunteering. For others, it is participating in fundraising events. Whatever they can do will help in building a strong community.

One year, we participated in the annual Owl Garden Party for the local Connecticut Audubon Society. It happened to be their 15th year, and they were giving out awards and recognitions to participants. My brother had taken his nephews off on one of the trails, and I was at a back-service table sampling something. Suddenly, the event director said she wanted to recognize and thank two men who had been helping her with the event since the very first day. I remember thinking,' I wonder who that could be? Probably the people who help her set up the event every year and then help with the cleanup afterward.' So, I was rather surprised when she called out our two names. Apparently, my brother and I represented the only restaurant to be involved for the entire 15 years. That event still goes on, and we are still a part of it – and plan to be a part as long as the event is held. It is part of our overall story of care and being active in our communities. That said, it is also nice to be recognized for our contributions.

A restaurant that takes a lead role in supporting its local community's many sub-communities will often find that those same groups will choose to help support them. This is true on all levels for any business. It does not have to be a restaurant, although they tend to be the most visible. I know of many people who have moved to a new area and have formed new social connections just by showing up to community events or being involved as a volunteer at these events.

We are all participants in various communities. By being more aware of them and by showing up and being involved with them and other people, we will all expand our own space of possibility. Who knows, you may find your future spouse at one, or your next business partner, or just about any meaningful relationship you may need or want.

Get involved, show up.

Aesthetics

"The aesthetics aren't merely a side note, they're as important as anything else." - Sylvain Neuvel

Aesthetics matter. They matter much more than many people think. Artists know this. Engineers know this. Designers know this. Car companies know this. How something looks – how it makes people feel when they see or interact with a person, place, or thing – matters to most of us, but many people forget to design for aesthetics in their businesses.

Many people do not even think about or even value how something looks and how it might make other people feel. Many people personalize aesthetics, thinking only about how they look or how their group of friends looks. Others put the emphasis only on the appearance of a thing and how that thing makes them feel. There is nothing wrong with any of this, but in a business, it is important in the design phase to create a place that people will enjoy. A place that will make them feel something, but then also do something: become a repeat customer. I have been in many restaurants where the aesthetics seem to have been an afterthought. I have been in many where the aesthetics seem to be the basis and the forefront of design.

All good restaurants work to create a memorable experience. This creation process starts even before the guest arrives. It exists in the story in the marketplace, in any marketing materials, and on the business's webpage and in social media. How it looks *before* the guest arrives for the first time is crucial. The experience continues once the customer enters the parking lot. Aesthetics matter here as well. The experience continues to the front door and the greeting. It also includes all other aspects of hospitality and design, from how the employees treat the guest, to how the restaurant is laid out, and what the customer sees from their seat. It includes how the menu is designed, the background music, the lighting, and oh-so-much more. It exists in all the details. The idiom *'The devil is in the details'* means that whatever one does should be done thoroughly and that the details are important. When we build or remodel a restaurant, I will often hear my brother voicing this idiom. Everything that we put into a design matters, and this always takes time and effort.

There is a story behind every detail in our restaurants, and while the customer will never know all the stories, it still matters. It matters because it creates the scene, it creates the mood, it creates and adds to the experience. It matters more than many people think.

The Vanilla Bean Café was built into an early nineteenth-century barn. During the remodel, we worked to keep the barn's integrity, enhance its beauty without overdoing it, and take away from the feeling that old wood creates. We exposed as many beams as possible and chose colors that helped emphasize their structure. We created a comfortable place where people could feel at home. One long-time customer says that during our weekend concerts, "With all the art on the walls and a glass of beer in hand, a show feels like a house concert in someone's living room." The Café is situated on the four corners of a bucolic New England hill town. A customer enters through the patio with a seasonal herb garden in front. All of this matters. We want the customer to feel comfortable and welcome before they even enter the building. Once inside, if the aesthetics are effective, magic happens.

One morning, a customer asked for the recipe for a muffin she had been enjoying. She told us it was one of the best muffins she had ever tasted. Since my mom told us to always tell the truth, I had to tell her that it was the most popular brand of scoop-and-bake muffin mix on the wholesale market. She had consumed that same muffin before in many other coffee shops and cafés. The difference was in the aesthetics. Though that muffin had been baked and served in the ordinary way – in our ovens, by our people, and served with our coffee – our environment, our overall aesthetics made the difference. It all matters! To that customer, her muffin tasted better because of the environment in which she was eating it, the story in which she was a valued character.

We did not create something new with aesthetics; it has been known for centuries. It is known by the best brands and used in movie making, in supermarket design, and at sporting events. A Boston Bruins hockey game would not be the same without the organ player. It matters how the customer feels, and aesthetics, good or bad, make feelings happen.

Have you been to a winery? These people know this and live and die by it. When visiting Sterling Vineyards, near Calistoga, California as part of a small VIP tour, a perk of owning a restaurant, the winery did something on the tour that I will never forget. I was in a group with a dozen other people: upscale liquor store owners, wine shop owners, and other restaurateurs. Near the end of the tour, we were taken into their wine cellar that housed the winery's best vintages. It was beautiful. The stonework, metalwork, beautiful woodwork, and lighting – all accented everything just perfectly. In that room, we were treated to what we were told was a great example of a specific vintage of wine. We were told the story of the year and what the vintners thought of that varietal. After we enjoyed our wine in the cellar, we were led upstairs to the grand tasting room that overlooks the valley and the hundreds of rows of grapevines. The first wine we were offered in this room was a wine of the same varietal but a different year. We were not told anything else about the wine. When we had all finished our sample, we were asked to compare the wine we had tasted in the cellar to the one we had just tasted and to give our overall assessment and declare which wine we preferred.

Everyone in the group declared that the wine in the cellar was the best one. Everyone except me, that is. When I had tasted the samples, I made a concerted effort to just taste the wine. I removed from play the different rooms in which we did the sampling and sought to remember only the two wines' flavor and feel. I judged the wine we had just tasted to be the superior wine. You must know here that I am no wine connoisseur. I like wine, I know a few varietals, and I can tell a good wine from a bad one. After years of cooking, what I have is a great palate for tasting things. We were all told that the wine we had tasted in the cellar was an exceptional wine, and it was very good. But after we had tasted the second sample in the tasting room and declared our preference, the vintners said they believed this one to be their best tasting wine of that varietal. The point they were making to us was that details, large and small – the room where you drink the wine, the story you tell about the experience – all matter in the customer's experience. Of course, experience is subjective, but the lesson here is an important one. By the way, the tour leader asked me why I chose the wine from the tasting room and not the cellar. I told them what I just told you. I tried to remove the overall experience and just taste the wines. They were impressed that I could do that (and yes – pat, pat – I just patted myself on the back).

I could literally write for days about the importance of the details. They matter. They matter in our personal appearance, in our homes, in our offices, and in all aspects of our daily lives. It matters in the interior of your car!

We go to great lengths to create a great and memorable experience for all our customers. Of course, not everyone is impressed. We had just finished the expansion of our bar at 85 Main, and the electrician and I were doing the final installation of the lights. I tend to go overboard with lighting, as I spent some time working in the theatre and believe that proper lighting makes or breaks a room. In the space of about ten minutes, this is what happened. We were just finishing a difficult and time-consuming installation when my electrician said to me, "You know what your problem is? You spend too much money and effort on lighting." I then stepped outside of the bar area to get a good look at what we had completed. A moment later, a customer waved me over to their table and said to me," You have done a great job in here. It looks beautiful. But you know what really makes it? The lighting." Case closed.

Of course, all of this is subjective. Another day, in the space of about ten minutes, one customer walked out saying our pricing was way too high. Another waved me over to his table to tell me that everything was great, from the staff and the vibe to the quality of the food and its presentation. Then he pointed at the menu – since it was his first time in the restaurant, he was re-reading it while he ate – and asked, "But how are you making any money with these prices?" I digress.

Aesthetics matter in how a place looks, but it also matters in how the employees look. That is why many places of employment institute a dress code or even require uniforms. How a person dresses tells a story. In many cases, this story is vital; think first responders or police uniforms. Investment bankers dress a certain way, and plumbers dress a certain way. It is all part of the story, and it is all related to aesthetics. An investment banker in sweatpants may not be someone with whom you want to deal (or they might be – depends on the overlying story). An auto mechanic with clean work clothes and clean hands tells a different story. People are advised to 'dress the part.' because this sends a message, and it helps to establish trust.

Many of the top-performing businesses in the hospitality industry have pleasing and recognizable uniforms. Not only does it help to build trust, but it is also a key part of their brand recognition; from hotels to airlines, we recognize these brands through their uniformed employees. These employers want all their employees to be recognizable as employees and proponents of the overall brand – hence the uniform – and the root of the word uniformity.

At our restaurants, we have different uniforms based on the offer of the restaurant. In our fast-casual establishments, we only require the service staff to be in branded t-shirts and the cooks to be in black cook shirts. The staff uniform is stricter at our upscale eatery with the staff in all black and the cooks in full chef coat and pants. How they dress tells the story, and it matters.

Of course, as the owner of four restaurants, you would think that I would dress in a way that identifies me as an owner. I do not. It is not important to the overall story that customers recognize me as the owner. When I fill a manager role, I will dress the part so that I am recognizable as a manager. My outfit in the winter is often jeans with a henley shirt. In the summer months, it is cargo shorts and a collared work shirt. The thing is, as an owner, I never know what work I will be doing on any given day. I could be in the office, I could be doing dishes, or I could be on my back attempting to fix a plumbing problem. Things break almost every day, and as the owner, I am often the person attempting to get it fixed. That is why I do not dress in my good clothes at work. One day, my wife saw me leaving for work in my standard look and said, "You should dress like you own four restaurants." I replied, "I do."

Of course, when I am going to restaurant-related events outside of my everyday work, I do my best to look the part of a restaurateur because the aesthetics matter in those situations.

Okay, assignment time. It is your turn to look for aesthetics; look for them everywhere you go. Try to gauge if they were planned or accidental or a combination somewhere between. Go through your day in a mood of wonder and be aware of how you feel based on how things look to you. Note your mood and any thoughts that might be triggered. Go to your favorite places and see if you can notice more about what makes it a favorite. Engage with the 'story' that is being told. You will notice what works well and what falls flat. You will learn what works for you and what does not. You may already know this, but this assignment will deepen it for you. My kids noticed this about me. They said when we are with mom, we go into places to shop. When we are with dad, we go in places just to look. This is just me doing my research work. You can do it, too.

The aesthetics you purposefully create are your own story manifested in visible reality through conversations and actions with others. Aesthetics matter, not just in a restaurant but in all aspects of your life, from how you dress to the outside of your house. Quality aesthetics have the capacity to make us feel better. When we feel better, we are capable of so much more.

Promises

"It's not what a person tells you that matters. It's how they treat you that reveals their true feelings. Their character is revealed not by the promises they make, but by the promises they keep."
- Anonymous

Once it has established itself as a business, the primary concern of any business is to STAY IN BUSINESS! All businesses make an offer or multiple offers; these offers are promises to fulfill (recurrently) that aim at customer satisfaction. We are only successful when our customers say they are satisfied, come back, and tell others about our product or service.

A business must keep existing customers and attract new ones to stay in business. To keep existing customers, we must continue to fulfill the promises that attracted them to us in the first place. Just by doing this, we can help take care of the second concern of staying in business: attracting new customers "Through word of mouth" from our existing customers who are satisfied with our offer will help attract new customers. This is why it is so important to keep the existing customer; they will attract the new ones.

A business owner hires employees to help fulfill the promises inherent in the business's offer. When a business owner makes the assessment that they need employees, they are saying that they cannot fulfill their offer by themselves anymore. They need help. The employer makes promises to the employee (i.e., pay, incentives, etc.), and the employee, in turn, makes a promise to the employer to help fulfill on the offer (or promise) of the business.

Employers make requests, and it is the job and promise of the employee to fulfill on those requests (as long as they are within the confines of the promise made by the business). For example, if you work in a shoe store, the employer cannot request that you make pizza deliveries. They can request that you wait on customers, take out the trash, clean the store, set up displays, and so on. Fulfilling requests (implicit or explicit), is the primary purpose of an employee. It is not up to the employee what requests they will fulfill and what ones they will not.

It all is simple and straightforward (or so it seems). In practice, you, the manager, may notice that your employees occasionally forget (or were never aware) that they have made a promise to take care of the offer made by the business. It is my experience that many employees get complacent in their specific jobs and get tunnel vision, becoming incapable of fulfilling on all aspects of their promise (within the scope of their training and education). What is worse, they act indignant when a request is made of them to take care of a concern well within the promise of the business. They become argumentative and difficult. They have a sense of entitlement to the way they are and the limits of what they do. In short, they become difficult to manage effectively. They become more of a cost than an asset. If they were a stock in a publicly traded company, I would dump them.

The Vanilla Bean Café (VBC) makes many promises that comprise its offer. This total offer is an experience we sell to the customer. All employees at the VBC promise to create and fulfill this experience for the customer. The experience will begin when a customer first hears about the VBC and makes plans to come for the first time. They drive in and 'see' the outside. Are the tables wiped and the chairs square? Is the patio clean? Is the garden in good shape? They may not ask these questions, but they will notice if things are not neat and clean. When they get inside, are they greeted by a warm and friendly atmosphere? Are the inside tables clear and wiped? Are the chairs square? Is the music appropriate? When they get to the counter, does a person who is bright, responsive, and attentive wait on them promptly? Again, while they are most likely not asking these questions, they will take note if something is "wrong" or does not please them.

In many cases, all it takes is one thing to be assessed as "wrong" to have a customer start looking for other things that may not meet their

Conditions of Satisfaction. Our goal is to not give them an opportunity to find one thing out of place. Most importantly and realistically, if they do find one thing, it will be difficult for them to find another.

Each customer who has a great experience will generate new customers by word of mouth. In most cases, they will be back, ensuring the survival of the business. By ensuring the customers' positive experience, from their first look at the place to the view of us in their rear-view mirror, we take care of the two conditions for staying in business. It is up to the employee to fulfill on this promise consistently and recurrently; this is because the reverse is also true. Each customer who has a bad experience will not be back and will not spread good words about the business. In fact, if employees do not take care consistently and recurrently, the dissatisfied customer may spread bad news about the place, hastening a possible demise of the business.

To most employees, this attention to the details seems pointless and easily forgotten or overlooked. To the owner of the business, it is in these details that existing and new customers are maintained and created. It is attention to these details that ensures the survival of the business and the continuation of employment for current and future employees.

A knowledgeable employee is one who embodies the knowledge necessary to consistently, recurrently, and effectively fulfill the promises made by the business – which, in turn, ensures the business's survival.

Collaboration

"Teamwork is the ability to work together toward a common vision. The ability to direct individual accomplishments toward organizational objectives. It is the fuel that allows common people to attain uncommon results." - Andrew Carnegie

I am the person I am today, not just because I showed up, but because many other people showed up at the same moment, in the same space. It is what we choose to do with those moments and those people that helps shape us into who we are becoming. This does not stop until we die. When you realize this, and act based on this understanding, the more you will have some control of situations and outcomes in your daily lives.

What made the other businesses and restaurants I have worked for and the restaurants I have opened much better learning experiences for my co-workers (and the customers) and me is that I have never tried to do it alone. They became better places, more effective places, due to the teamwork and collaboration that helped to initiate and foster.

To some people, teamwork has become a cliché. Just walk into any office, and you will see the posters, the ones that are often made fun of and parodied to the point where they lose their message. Teamwork is crucial to achieve any goal effectively. Nothing teaches you that like a busy Saturday night in a popular restaurant. The coordination and collaboration necessary just to set up for that night is extensive and vital. If prepped properly, or as we say in the business, 'setup for success' a busy night will appear smooth and easy to the customer or casual observer, and only those in the know will understand what it truly takes to make it look so easy.

One of our restaurants is located next to The University of Connecticut. Move-in weekend is one of our busiest times of the year with thousands of students, parents, and families descending on the campus during a short period of time. Our restaurant will serve over 4,000 people during that weekend. It is through planned, coordinated effort that our staff makes this look easy. It begins the week before when we look at our history and make a projection about the upcoming weekend. We coordinate with our suppliers and our prep team on what we will be needing and how best to accomplish the numerous tasks to be completed. We provide six soups and three chilis every day that weekend; just coordinating these can be a difficult task. Then there are the 40-plus other menu items that need to be prepped and executed efficiently.

On top of that, we have a smoothie bar and barista station that will handle hundreds of orders each day. When you take the time to consider the amount of work that needs to be completed, it seems overwhelming. Yet, we succeed through proper management, communication, and collaboration to make a crazy weekend into something easily managed and satisfying for our customers as well as our staff. We are so good at this that our staff looks forward to this weekend every year because of how satisfying it is for us to pull it off, to see so many happy customers, and have fun along the way.

Legendary business guru, Brian Tracy, has this to say about Teamwork, "Teamwork is so important that it is virtually impossible for you to reach the heights of your capabilities or make the money that you want without becoming very good at it." We strive for this in each of our restaurants. If you have ever worked in the restaurant industry, you know the joy of a well-run and cohesive operation and the misery of one that is poorly run. The difference between the two is obviously better management. When you break that management down into its parts, it is the emphasis on teamwork and clear communication of goals that make all the difference. A well-run establishment creates a happy workforce, and a happy workforce with clear instructions working together to achieve a goal is magical to watch. We have customers who visit our restaurants to do just that. They love to watch the interaction of our staff and how well they accomplish their tasks, all while providing top-level hospitality. It is a joy to watch from my perspective as well.

I approach collaboration in most things that I do in the same way that I make a new soup. I start with an idea, or perhaps I have been inspired by something I may have eaten recently. I may also be using leftovers to create something that will be one of a kind. In the latter case, I begin by assembling my leftovers and imagine what I could make with the assortment that I have before me. I will engage in a discussion with other cooks, or I may just begin and later seek their input. Either way, their input is important. Each cook will approach the new recipe from their own experience and perspective, also with a knowledge of what other ingredients we have on hand. Ingredients may be added or subtracted until we reach an agreed upon recipe. I then set about to make the soup and, though I sometimes ask for input while I am in the process, I will always ask for input at the end to find ways to tweak the flavors so that they are all balanced with the 'theme' of the soup being forward. For example, if it were a Mexican-flavor soup, we would want those flavors to be what is tasted first with other ingredients complementing the forward flavors, supporting them, allowing a finish, or final taste, to be lasting and memorable on many levels. Who knew soup could be so complex? And Fun! Once it is complete and we really like it, I may write the final recipe should we attempt to reproduce it a second time.

Over the years, I have made thousands of soups, and there are many that have been committed to writing. After writing a recipe, I make the soup again, following exactly what I have written, and then with input from others, I tweak the seasonings to adjust the flavor to achieve the profile I am looking for. That achieved, I rewrite the recipe and have a prep cook make the soup following exactly this revised recipe. If they can create the same soup, and it is what we call a 'winner,' 'the recipe is then added to our recipe book.

This same collaboration approach has been used each time I have renovated a space or built an entirely new restaurant. It starts with a thought (usually mine – but not always) that gets turned into a conversation. That conversation will then become a drawing and a business plan. Each of these steps requires collaboration with other professionals, from builders to bankers to architects. We then turn these ideas into start-up money to complete the task; this also requires collaboration. Once the drawings are complete and the building permit secured, the building process begins. Collaboration continues at every stage. I rely on the input from the professionals to help me make the concept even better and complete the project. Their knowledge combined with my willingness to change when something just right is presented helps to create a much better restaurant than if I had just plowed ahead with my original ideas and vision alone. Input will sometimes come from unexpected places and people, so it is important to pay attention and be ready to learn something new every day you are on the job.

At one restaurant, there was a large support pole right in the middle of the space. In the early design stages, I did my best to work around the pole so it would not be in the way of the kitchen and service area. When I presented my initial sketches to the architect, along with my story about the space, they presented me with a new idea for the support pole. The main architect told me that he saw it as a design element, while I saw it as a problem to overcome. With his interpretation, he was able to incorporate the support pole in such a way that it became a centerpiece and made the support pole almost invisible.

When we were near completion, and I was deciding on finishes wall coverings, what color to paint the upper portion of the 3' diameter support one of my prep cooks, who just happened to be visiting that day, said to me, "Why not just wrap it in the same stuff you use to make the blackboards?" A flat black formica. It was brilliant! We did what she suggested, and it became not only our soup and chili board but also a kiosk where we could communicate with our customers and employees.

It is through willful collaboration with professionals along with encouraging and appreciating the input from others around me that what I work to create becomes much better than if I had just done it my way. This is true in all aspects of our lives. It is perhaps the number one reason that people get married – because "together we are more" – *Maria Sangiolo,* my wife.

Working with others can be chaotic at times, but learning to embrace the chaos and allow it to unfold naturally can yield some surprising results. Creative growth comes from taking risks and from going somewhere new with an open mind along with other people who are currently on the same page. Collaborating with others is not always easy, as Bono, the lead singer of U2, the world-renowned Irish rock band from Dublin, has said: "When we're making the records, it always feels a bit like we're drowning, and you do wonder if there's an easier way. But we seem to need some chaos to bring us together." Embrace the difficulty of working and collaborating with others and accept the chaos that can come with it. It will increase the possibilities and the potential of any project.

So, learn to collaborate, learn to be an effective team member, learn to not 'go it alone.' Everything that you touch with intention combined with positive input from other dedicated members of your team will become ever so much more than what you started out with or what you thought you could achieve before you began. Let collaboration become a hallmark of your entire life.

Competition

"A flower does not think of competing with the flower next to it, it just blooms." - Zen Shin

There is this notion that businesses are in competition with other businesses. I find this idea misses the mark. Such competition takes away from the time, energy, and resources we could be expending on improving our offer. This is also true for each of us as individuals. We are not in competition with anyone. In business, our competition is us and our last year's performance. We strive to be better than we were in the past. The same is also true personally. I strive to be a better version of who I was last year. Whether in business or as an individual self, it is simply a waste of time to be in a declared state of competition.

Of course, some things have been brought into existence solely for competition. Sports are a good example. Even at the highest competitive levels, the best coaches emphasize becoming a better team than they were last year. The best individual team members prioritize becoming a better version of themselves to benefit the team goal of becoming a better team.

Some restaurants appear to be in competition. I like to think of it more as a rivalry. 'Competition' is focused on one's competitors and winning, while rivalry is about a relationship in which different businesses work side by side to keep their shared market alive and profitable. A good example is McDonald's and Burger King. I do not see them as being in competition, as each entity works at always improving its own offer. They are rivals in the sense that they have very similar offers in the same market of consumers. While these restaurants sometimes take friendly jabs at each other, the main focus of each is on improving their own business and attracting more customers. You can call that competition if you want, but competition's fixation on winning leads only to wasted time, energy, and resources. Rivalry seems more fun.

The same is true when it comes to pizza. You can get pizza in just about any town in America. Many towns have more than one pizza joint. Are they in competition? We can certainly look at it that way and say that they are competing against each other for a limited number of customers who want pizza on any given day. Maybe some of the owners see it that way, but I think it would be better for everyone to look at it differently and see each pizza shop as working simply to become the best version of itself. This would benefit the pizza market, as well as each company's employees and customers. It encourages all pizza joints to create effective actions to take care of their businesses better.

Sam Walton (founder of Wal-Mart) said, "Control your expenses better than your competition. This is where you can always find the competitive advantage." This speaks directly to focusing on the business rather than the perceived competition.

We often hear that wild animals are in competition for food, and the definition of competition certainly allows for this use of the word. But this is not the way that we humans think of competition; we compete for trophies and banners, while the wild animals are only interested in survival for themselves and their families and/or groups. They will only fight when they must, as fighting is a waste of time, energy, and resources. That time could be better spent hunting to take care of their survival or resting for the next hunt.

When you think about anything as being a competition, you wind up engaging in activities that are wasteful. It is best to focus on using your time to create a better version of yourself, your business, your family, etc., without wasting energy on winning a perceived competition.

As in sports, having a business competitor can be a motivating factor. If thinking that you are in a competition motivates you to be a better version of yourself and to work at creating the best possible version of your business, then, by all means, enjoy the competition. Just make sure it is not too costly.

I am not saying do not pay attention to what other businesses are doing. Indeed, it is a good way to learn. The restaurant industry has been called an industry of thieves because there is little a restaurateur enjoys more than visiting other restaurants to steal ideas. The newer version of that is going online and checking out other restaurants' menus and specials for inspiration or for outright theft. Learning from others is how we all get along. I am sure that the restaurant industry is not the only thieving industry, but this industry seems to be quite blatant about its actions.

It is also true for us as individuals; we learn from seeing what other people are doing. It becomes a problem when, rather than using others as inspiration to mobilize us to become better versions of ourselves, we stop being individuals and start copying. This can become a pathology; consider the words of a Madonna fan when asked why she copycat-dresses like Madonna, "We are just trying to express our individuality."

Be inspired by others. Be mobilized into action by what others are doing. Do not waste time with feelings of inadequacy or jealousy and comparing yourself to 'the competition.' Take action to be a better you. Life is not a competition.

Understanding Business

"One of the most important areas we can develop as professionals is competence in accessing and sharing knowledge." - Connie Malamed

I wrote a paper on the knowledge one needs to open and run a restaurant effectively. I wrote it to help me understand the business in a deeper way so that I could be more effective in my role. I also wrote the paper to share with others who choose to be in the restaurant business. I will go over how to apply my thinking to other domains of knowledge that one will need for success in any business.

Here is an excerpt from my paper. The complete piece is in the Appendix:

A great restaurant creates an illusion for the average customer that running a restaurant can be all very easy. This may be one of the reasons so many people want to open restaurants. They believe that they can easily achieve what a great restaurant does consistently and recurrently through years of practice. I have noticed that the restaurant business is a business of non-professionals; by this I mean that anyone can open a restaurant. You do not even have to have any prior knowledge (imagine that). This is not true of most other professions. Subsequently, many people have no idea what they are in for when they open a new restaurant. I also find that most people are unwilling to ask for help – a recipe for disaster that helps the nation have an 50-60% failure rate for restaurants within their first two years of operation.

If you are going to open and/or run a new restaurant, you had better have a lot of prior knowledge in the industry (or be willing to pay for someone else to provide the knowledge). I make the claim that the restaurant business requires skills in six separate and permanent areas of knowledge (domains). The first domain is the obvious; you must know about food, and there is a lot to know about food, including all there is to know about food safety. Passion about food is not required, but it sure helps to love what you are doing (why are you doing this anyway?). The second also seems obvious, and that is what I call customer relations, or having good people skills. This is the hospitality industry, and that requires taking care of people and their concerns, repeatedly, in an effective manner. You want the customer to feel a sense of comfort up to and beyond their expectations in order to produce in them a willingness to return (again and again) with service provided in such a way that they tell their friends and family about their experience. The third domain of knowledge is that of retail sales. This is a retail business where we have goods and services for sale, and to complicate matters, the goods are perishable. The Gap does not have this problem; those sweaters are not going to go bad and start stinking up the storeroom. This requires a fourth domain of knowledge: the handling and processing of perishable items. This requires a specific, non-standard retail skill set. It is important to order just what you need and have practices for using everything before it can no longer be used effectively (i.e., it must be thrown out or you will poison someone). The fifth domain of knowledge needed is in finance. This includes back-office accounting, year-end accounting, payroll, cash flow, capital improvements, and cash handling. This is not just about counting the money. This is a crucial area if you want to fully understand how business works and function effectively in that business. The final domain of necessary knowledge is in marketing. Every business owner should have this as one of their primary concerns. How do you get people through your doors consistently while continuously attracting new customers? Good question.

This claim of six separate domains of knowledge is by no means complete and could be added to (I do not believe that it can be subtracted from) based on individual operations. Some additions would fall under one of the six domains that I have put forth above, for example, employee relations. I would put this under customer relations because your employees are also your customers, and you need to know how to work with them consistently and effectively. You also need to know how to get rid of employees you do not want – and you will (most likely) have more than a few of them.

Six Domains of Knowledge

1.   Food
2.   *Customer Relations*
3.   *Retail Sales*
4.   *Manufacturing*
5.   *Finance*
6.   *Marketing*

Most of us cannot work effectively in all the six domains listed above, and we need help from others to fulfill on our offer of a quality dining experience. This help can be a partner, hired employees, or outside services. It is important to know what it is that you can do well and when you need to hire other people to help you cover all the domains well. No one person can take care of all the concerns listed above effectively and still take care of the many concerns not related to work (i.e., marriage, friendships, play, family, etc.).

Of the six domains of knowledge listed above, most businesses that are not restaurants or food manufacturing oriented will not need knowledge about food. The first domain listed can be changed to whatever product or service the company offers. In the restaurant's case, it happens to be food.

One area I left out of my original paper is the domain of play or fun. I firmly believe that we must cultivate a fun work environment for all the people with whom we interact, be they employees, co-workers, vendors, or customers. So, let us add Fun to the list.

Some other areas of knowledge include: Technology, Ethics, Leadership, Membership, Planning, Education, Politics, and Fun. This list is adapted from the book by Fernando Flores,

Conversations for Action and Collected Essays: Instilling a Culture of Commitment in Working.

Let us look briefly at each one and get a better understanding of how to incorporate these domains into our work-life.

Technology – I should have listed this in my earlier paper on restaurants. Times have changed. It is much more important now to keep up with the technology that serves the business sector that you will be functioning within.

Ethics – How will you or your business behave in the world? This a deep area and would need multiple chapters to explore in detail. Suffice it to say that behaving ethically is important for any person or business that plans on a long and prosperous future. Sadly, there are people who behave unethically who also do seem to do well.

Leadership – Learning how to lead people is a primary area of knowledge if you want to have successful teams and a successful business.

Membership – We are members of the National Federation of Independent Businesses as well as the Connecticut Restaurant Association. It is important to engage in membership, as these organizations are in existence to be partners in our operation. They pay attention to larger areas of concern that we may not have time with which to engage.

Planning – Planning is an important part of any viable business. It is also important for any individual. Taking time to plan a future, to basically tell a story about what you believe you will accomplish, goes a long way in creating the desired outcome. If I did not engage in effective planning, I would have a hard time running a restaurant, let alone designing and building three others.

Education – Continuing education is vital for all aspects of any operation. Business is changing rapidly, and continuing your education keeps you informed and knowledgeable to adapt to changing conditions.

Politics – Sadly, yes, politics plays into all our lives. Paying attention and even actively being engaged in politics will help you to navigate potential problems along your path. You may also find that, at times, politics and ethics will present themselves as two peas in a situational pod. This will require of you a discerning quality of attention.

Fun – All I can say here is that you must engage each day with a sense of playfulness and fun to keep the good work from becoming too stressful and unenjoyable.

All these areas of concern are important to engage with when operating a business. If you do not have the knowledge, it is best to hire or outsource people that do have the necessary knowledge. That will allow you the time to focus on the aspects of the business that are important to you, vital for cash flow, and necessary for the sustainability and durability of the business. A good practice would be to write all these concerns, list action plans in each one, and assign a person who will be responsible for their completion. That practice will go a long way in creating a viable business. Ideally, you want to run the business, not have the business run you.

Profitability

"Profit is not a cause but a result."
- Peter F. Drucker

As Peter Drucker points out, profit is a result. It is the outcome of actions in two different domains, sales and finance. You must increase sales and reduce costs to produce a profit. This is profit in its simplest form, but it is the result of so much more.

In the restaurant business, profit results from our overall offer, from the menu and service to the overall ambiance to our quality of product. All this produces cost; the cost of any business with a physical location can be very high. Add to that, a restaurant needs a lot of employees to fulfill on the offer. Those two areas are referred to in the restaurant industry as the Prime Cost: 65% of total cost. This prime cost is Costs of Goods Sold and Labor plus Fringe (workers' compensation insurance, social security, unemployment taxes, etc.). That leaves the remainder of 35% to cover all other costs of business, including rent, insurance, heat, electricity, advertising, credit card fees, etc. All these costs put the squeeze on the profit department. They are referred to as fixed costs. There is not much you can do to change them, and small changes do not do much to increase profit. For example, saving $30 per month on a phone bill may only create $360 additional dollars of profit. Prime Costs are the area in which we have the most control over our profitability. Engaging in effective practices in ordering, scheduling, product management, and day-to-day management of labor can go a long way toward increasing profitability to the tune of tens of thousands of dollars. It is a matter of knowing where to put your attention and energies to create the most return on your investment.

Other businesses have their metrics for Costs of Goods Sold, Labor, etc. No matter the business you are working within, find out what those metrics are and where you can take action to create profit.

Businesses are created to fulfill on some product or service that is needed in the marketplace. While their primary focus is to fulfill on that offer, a business also needs to be viable and sustainable; this includes making a profit. All employees are responsible for helping to generate a profit. The problem comes when they are not told that this it is part of their job description.

When employees feel like they are an integral part of a business, they will work more effectively in their day-to-day tasks. It is important for employers to stress this in the onboarding and continuing education of all employees.

I have learned that there are three different kinds of employees: Cost Producers, Income Producers, and Profit Producers. Cost Producers are there to fulfill on a task that does not generate income and does not generate profit. In a restaurant, an example of a Cost Producer is the cleaning company. Income Producers are the sales force. An example from the restaurant industry would be waitstaff and bartenders. Profit Producers are the people who can act in the two domains of Sales and Finance effectively. They can increase sales either through promotions and increased customer traffic, or increased per person spending, and also by encouraging repeat business. These could be managers or waitstaff and bartenders. They are also very good at controlling costs. These people could be chefs who utilize every item that comes through the door in an effective way and managers who effectively control the labor costs on a day-to-day basis.

All that said, I like to think of all employees as Income Producers. Each person's job is integral to the operation. Otherwise, we would not have them as an employee. Including them in conversations about sales and profit can only be a good thing for the business. Without a good dishwasher, a restaurant comes to a grinding halt. A dishwasher who knows how to prioritize and keep the kitchen functioning smoothly can be an Income Producer. A dishwasher who can work effectively without breaking dishes and glassware is a cost-cutter. Teach them about water costs and conservation; watch them use less water and still achieve their desired outcome.

Treat every member of the team as integral to the business's profitability, and you will have a more profitable business. Teach them how the business operates and share the business financials with those who have an interest and care.

Then there's profit that is not balance sheet related. To think of profit as only cash in the bank is extremely limiting and too narrow a definition for a truly successful business. A business owner can realize a profit from a business in many ways that are not cash in the bank. Some examples include: achieving a balanced lifestyle, a healthy community, healthy employees, a happy workplace, open time for family, friends, play, and many other life goals. Cash profit is only one desired result. A well-run business can create many other valuable 'life-profits' for yourself and for those who work with you. Doing so distinguishes a merely profitable business from one that is truly successful.

Situations

"It's not the situation, but whether we react negative or respond positive to the situation that is important." - Zig Ziglar

We all find ourselves in situations every day. Some situations are positive and help create effective outcomes and futures. Some situations are negative and can foster breakdowns throughout an organization. Some situations are neutral or normal and could be considered general operational situations.

The practice of thinking about the situations in your daily life as you are moving through them helps you to recognize when you are in one that is not working for you. It could be something in your personal life or a situation at work. When you recognize you are in one that needs to change, pay attention to the action(s) you choose while you are attempting to reorganize the situation. After you have engaged in an action of change, ask yourself, "Did that work? Am I in a more advantageous or desirable situation? Or did that make things worse?" It is important to notice, to take a hard look at what you attempted and achieved, and to determine whether it worked satisfactorily or not.

In the chapter on Good Bad/Right Wrong, we noted that people do not learn from their mistakes. They learn from being aware that they made a mistake and then being willing to look at the mistake with a commitment to improving. It starts with being aware, with noticing. The same holds true for undesirable situations if you want to engage in action to change them to effective situations. The skill of noticing and taking action to make desirable changes in your current situations is crucial to improving your actions and outcomes in the future.

One Sunday at one of the restaurants, we ran into staffing difficulty and were short one breakfast cook to fulfill our offer properly. The manager on duty instructed a member of the staff to improve the situation. The result was that the staff person felt personally attacked and blamed for the problem. And she walked out! Looking back at that exchange, the manager on duty told me that the only thing they could hear was my voice in their head, "Are you in a better situation or a worse one?" From that point on, that manager grew to be more effective in situation management. It did not happen overnight, but the seed that had been planted through education had taken root through engagement and reflection.

When you find yourself in a situation and, based on your assessment, you declare it to be unsatisfactory, keep your overall story in mind as you engage in action to change the situation to a more effective and harmonious one. Then look at the outcome and see if the actions you engaged in were successful. If not, what can you learn to improve for the future? Making assessments of our actions in life's situations is how we all go through life, but by making situation management a deliberate, recurrent practice, you can become much more effective in a shorter time frame.

Situation management is not an easy practice to make routine, and we often end the day in bed thinking of things we could have done differently. That is okay. This is learning. Cultivating your ability to notice with a desire for change is a great beginning. Just continue to make this practice a part of your story, and you will find that you will improve over time.

Be The Storyteller

"The universe is made of stories, not of atoms."
- Muriel Rukeyser

My job is not to motivate. My job is to mobilize. Motivation requires me to take an active role to effect change inside another person's head. (Good luck!) Mobilization requires me to tell a compelling story that attracts the right people, a story that fits the employee's own life story and the direction they are going in their life. My job is to create a space of attractive possibilities to a potential employee, a place where they activate their own motivation to be a top performer. My job as a storyteller is to create a place of attractive possibilities to a potential employee, a space in which they want to act effectively - mostly for themselves - but also for the business. I must also be a good actor within my own story. I must live it so they can see it. I must be living and telling my story every day. Perhaps you have heard this said as 'Walk the Talk.'

Developing a narrative that is compelling and rewarding is what we all are working to do with our own lives. It is what all business owners are attempting to do through their business marketing, always with varying degrees of success.

Developing your own narrative about your own life is also a vital skill. This is where the language as a verb begins to resonate. You want to create a story about your life that is like that of a business; it must be compelling and rewarding. It must attract other people to you who like being a part of your unfolding saga. It must create value for yourself and others. It is a good idea to take the time and compose your story. Begin by just imagining the next year. Then the next five years, then the next ten. All stories take place in the imagination first. They must begin with a thought and then be put into words and then into action.

As part of an education class I took in the late 90s, I had to write my own personal 'business plan.' It was my story of how I expected my life to turn out. I have revisited this plan a number of times to update it and change or revise it based on how things were turning out. While it did not turn out exactly as I had written it, that business plan did act as a guide that helped me to make decisions throughout my life. You, too, may want to write out your own business plan (or desired life narrative).

Canadian-American motivational public speaker and self-development author, Brian Tracy, has this to say about the number one habit of successful people, "The first habit is to become goal-oriented. You need to be a habitual goal setter and dedicate yourself to working from clear, written goals every day of your life, forming daily habits. All highly successful people are intensely goal-oriented. They know exactly what they want, they have it written down, they have written plans to accomplish it, and they both review and work on their plans as a daily routine." They have it written down. While they may not see it as a story, setting goals is part of your story, and when you take the time to write them down, it is much more real and easier to manifest in your life.

This writing down of your story can be thought of as a life plan, like a business plan, but for the life you wish to create. It could be a practice that you revisit each year, or you could revisit it every five years. The point is to have a story about your future and be open of modifying it as goals and situations change. They do change, and you do want to be able to adapt your story to the changes.

Your story is much bigger than a life plan. It contains all that you care about: your ideas, opinions, philosophies, and your story of your past. Oddly enough, you are not entitled to know what you care about. You can only find out through meaningful conversations with others, through reflective thinking and writing. Sometimes we are often surprised to learn about something we care about because it shows up to us through our life experiences. For example, you may not know you care about support for people who are disabled in some way until you are friends with someone who is, and you learn more about their life and what they care about.

You must engage life with others in meaningful conversations to discover more about who you are and what you care about. From that, you can develop your story to include more meaning and more depth. Your stories shape who we are and who we are becoming. Your own story about ourselves shapes our future. Your story shapes how you show up to others, and that has a direct effect on how others interact with you. Or, as *author and journalist Francesco Marconi put it,* "Stories shape how others see you and could have implications for whether you are hired, go on dates, or even raise money for your next business idea."

To illustrate how you tell your story with your actions and the consequences that are produced, it will be helpful to see how it can also work against you. Many years ago, we had an employee who was a victim of his culture (aren't we all in varying degrees). By that, I mean that he had chosen to dress a certain way, wear his hat sideways, and own a fast car. That look attracted a certain girlfriend who was just trouble. He kept on lamenting how he kept getting stopped by the police, and that life was unfairly difficult for him. My brother would often tell him, "Lose the hat, the car, and the girlfriend, and your life will improve." For a while, he did not heed my brother's advice. He left our employ and went on to work at other restaurants. His travels brought him back to us for a short time, and he was a changed person. He said to me, "you know what, your brother was right." The last I heard from him he was the executive chef at small restaurant group in the Hartford area. The lesson here: your story, and how you embody it, matters.

Your narrative is an important part of the life you are working to create. Take the time to write it down and revisit it often, and always make sure it is adaptable to change.

Part 4 – Commitment

"Commitment is an act, not a word."
- Jean-Paul Sartre

"Commitment is what transforms a
promise into a reality."
- Abraham Lincoln

Learning for Life

"Live as if you were to die tomorrow. Learn as if you were to live forever." - Mahatma Gandhi

Throughout our lives, we are constantly in a place where we can be learning something new. This is true from the moment we are born to the moment we die. In this infinite universe that is always changing, it only stands to reason that there is always something new to learn. Learning in the early years of life is not a choice. It happens on a biological level independent of our thinking mind. It appears that once our formal education is complete and we enter the job market, many people only learn what they must learn to remain employed and keep food on the table. At the other end of this spectrum are the naturally curious people who continue their education in countless ways. These people educate themselves in many areas of their lives and act with the knowledge they acquire to help them live a more fulfilled and meaningful life.

The vast majority of people are in the middle of this range; they learn for their job and also continue to learn outside their job through reading and discussing with others about many areas of their lives. There is a disconnect: many people in this mid-range do not then engage in effective action, so what they are learning never makes a significant difference in their lives. Reading, discussion, and casual conversation are not enough. You must make it real by adopting practices that create a new way of living.

A good example of this can be seen in the book *The Four Agreements: A Practical Guide to Personal Freedom (A Toltec Wisdom Book)* by Don Miguel Ruiz, first published in 1997; it is still popular today. Many people I know have read the book, and it has been recommended to me numerous times. It has been called a life-changing book, and it can be. But YOU must do something about it other than just read it. When I ask people who have read the book what The Four Agreements are, most recall only one. That one agreement resonated with who they were then and where they were in their own personal development. It made sense to them. Then time passed, and they read many other books, and they forgot about the other agreements in Ruiz's book. We think we know a book just because we read it, but we lose it shortly after reading it. The only way to retain the wisdom offered in the book is to live into it deliberately. Talk about it with others, yes. Form a book discussion group, yes. But also write about it yourself in a journal, re-read the book at least two more times, listen to it on CD, etc. These are ways to deepen the wisdom offered in the book and make it part of your thinking. Once this is achieved, actions follow. Most people do not get this far. Most people think they are learning when they are not. If something resonates with you, find ways to build it in your thinking, language, and, most importantly, actions. This is how information becomes knowledge.

The information in The *Four Agreements* is akin to what we teach the employees at our restaurants. So, if you are familiar with that book, you likely will find some correlations between it and what you read in this book.

I have found that just being curious and making an attempt to live in a mood of wonder helps me to seek out new answers and continue my education. I find that I can learn from people around me, including my employees and partners.

Just by being engaged in conversation with a stranger can lead me down a path that I want to learn more about. That is an excellent thing about the hospitality industry. I am constantly engaging with strangers.

Learning something new is so much easier today than it has ever been. I know countless people who have learned by watching YouTube videos, myself included. I recently learned the Tai Chi Yang Style 32 Sword Form from watching videos on YouTube, along with deepening my knowledge by reading more about it and Tai Chi in general, both online and in books.

Making a commitment to learning for life will help to create a brighter future for yourself and others around you. Remember to make it Fun.

Profit in Life

"Of all the things that can have an effect on your future, I believe personal growth is the greatest. We can talk about sales growth, profit growth, asset growth, but all of this probably will not happen without personal growth." - Jim Rohn

What is profit? How do you make it? If I ask you to go out and make a profit, what would you do? It is not really an actionable request like, 'make a sandwich' or 'make a garden.' It is clear what needs to be done when you make a sandwich or a garden. You can think about what steps need to be taken and completed to create the desired outcome. When asked to make a profit, the steps to take are not as clear or ready to act upon. The reason for this is that a profit is created by action in two different areas. In business, those areas are 'increase sales' and 'decrease expenses.'

If I ask you to increase sales, you can think of actionable practices in which you can engage in to do this. For example, you might want to have a sale or extend your hours or even expand the offer to include other product lines. At the same time, if I ask you to decrease expenses, you can again think of areas in which you could take action. You might start by looking at an expense report to see where savings might be possible. The point is that to produce a profit, you must be thinking about action in two different areas. The same holds true for yourself and the future you are working to produce; you can make your work profitable for your life, now and in the future.

"How so?" you ask.

By creating a more valuable or profitable future you. To create this more profitable future you, you must engage today in effective action in two different areas (but you knew that, didn't you?). The first is by increasing knowledge; this is analogous to increasing sales. You should maximize your own on-the-job learning. Think of your job as an educational facility. Learn as much as you can from everyone with whom you work. In my experience, people who know things almost always love to teach them to an interested pupil. Be that interested pupil. Always. A job is never just a job; it is a place of abundant learning. If you choose to see it this way, you should always be learning something new. Of course, there are jobs that are not this. If you find yourself in one, look for another job.

The second way to create a more profitable future yourself is by "decreasing your expenses." By this, I mean minimizing your negative and self-destructing habits and thoughts and getting free of all the 'stuff' that gets in the way of your learning and creating a more effective and valuable future you. Ineffective habits are easier to see than ineffective thoughts; both will take significant effort to change. Examples of ineffective habits include: being consistently late, not getting enough sleep, excessive use of alcohol or other drugs, not treating others with respect, etc. You know the negative thoughts: 'I can't do that' or 'I'm not smart enough' or 'I'll never learn that.' These are all self-destructive and true only because you 'think' they are true. They are the roadblocks that you (or someone else) put there and that you believe to be the truth. There is no doubt that these thoughts are your 'truths,' but they can be changed. We all have the ability to change our thoughts; it happens by practicing mindfulness and engaging in new thoughts that take care of us. Though we all learn at different speeds and in different ways, every one of us has the ability to continue learning and growing and changing. (By the way, traditional school is NOT for everyone. The traditional school is designed to take care of the administration and the teachers. Rarely is it designed to take care of the student. If it were designed for the student, teenagers would not be required to be at school at 7:30 am.) Do not let the experiences you had with learning in school be an indicator of the kind of learner you are or can be. When it comes to embodied learning, or what I call knowledge, you have to learn by doing. When I say doing, I mean doing something over and over again with a deepening understanding each time (recursion). Knowledge is what professionals get paid for. You can keep learning, find your own way, and keep doing it.

While you are employed anywhere, keep saying 'yes' to learning new and different jobs; this is your 'increase sales' domain. Always be in a mood of wonder. Strive to learn anything new that resonates with you and points toward the future you are working to produce. To decrease your 'expenses,' become aware of your self-destructive thoughts and practice new self-assuring ones. Do not associate with your self-defeating thoughts; watch them rise and let them go. Then immediately engage in a positive thought. Start small and work up to more self-strengthening thoughts. Remember, like anything that we learn, this takes time. You did not learn how to ride your bike by reading about it. You had to get on it, and you had to practice every day. You most likely fell off a number of times, and our teacher likely expected we would. "Falling" should be expected every time we try something new with our body. It is the natural way. It takes time to train the body to do something new, and your mind is generated in part by the body that you are, along with the things that you practice. Be gentle with yourself and know that this ride you are on is a long one. If you work at it and believe that you can, a more profitable you will be found further down the road.

↑   Increase Learning and Education
↓   Decrease Negative and Ineffective
    Thoughts and Habits
→   = a More Profitable You

"You are today where your thoughts have brought you; you will be tomorrow where your thoughts take you." - James Lane Allen, American novelist

Language is a Verb - Part 2

"We are what we think. All that we are arises with our thoughts. With our thoughts we make the world." - Buddha Dhammapada

"The world is what we make it." This statement should seem more true to you than when you began reading this book. If you have already learned this truism along your path, it should not seem that strange now. Every day we generate our world from our thoughts as we use language and choose the actions in which we engage. We co-create this world with all the people we work with and all the people that we never meet. There are people who are much better at generating reality for vast numbers than other people. Think of Twitter. In the last century, that was a sound a bird made. Now it is something with which millions of people around the world interact every day. There is a new reality that did not exist before. It was created and shared in language. Think of Apple Computer. Think of any person or organization that has changed the world in which we live. You will see that they do it with language. They can only do it with language. Language that turns into action helps to manifest our world and world view.

This knowledge is power. You have power; we all have power. When you use your language knowing you are helping to create, you tend to make wiser choices with the words you use. This quotation by the international speaker and author, Yehuda Berg, reflects on the power that our words contain, "Words have energy and power with the ability to help, to heal, to hinder, to hurt, to harm, to humiliate, and to humble."

When I think about all that I have created throughout my life, I can look back on tasks, events, and restaurants (!) and see that it was my ability to communicate clearly that enabled me to accomplish what I have been able to accomplish. I can also look back and see some of the damage I have done by not understanding the power of my spoken words. As with anything with which we engage and can observe, there is a balance that can be achieved. I do not succeed at everything., nor do I always take care of all I want to take care of with my actions. There have been times when I have made changes in my business to ensure survival, and someone lost their job. While it was necessary to continue with what I do to fulfill on my offers and take care of my customers and employees, I cannot always create a space for everyone's success. It is not possible.

Nor is it possible to be effective every time. Many times, my words have not been enough, sometimes what was said caused more problems than they solved. The main thing is to keep doing, pick up the pieces, and keep moving.

I strive for balance in my life when I use my words. I work to create positivity and reduce negativity with the words I choose. I am an optimist at heart and will always look for the positive and good in any interaction. I choose my words carefully and work with my managers, employees, and my own children to be mindful of the words they use that have the possibility to open or close different futures for them. I recently was working with an employee to encourage her to take on more responsibility and learn a new skill. Her response? "I can't do that. I tried it once." Every time I hear someone say that they cannot do something, my internal come back is, "If you say so." With those words, they shut down future possibilities. They have drawn a line in the sand. When someone says that they cannot do a particular thing, it limits not only conversation but the future. They limit themselves and what may be possible for them. At the time, I pointed out to her the limiting power of her words and suggested she reframe her response to something like, "I have tried that before and didn't do well, but I am willing to make another attempt." Again, for the sake of redundancy, these are the words of Henry Ford, founder of Ford Motor Company: *"Whether you believe you can or not, you're right."*

Another example of a word that is limiting and creates an exit strategy for the speaker is the word 'try.' When I hear an employee tell me that they will 'try' to do something, I point at some small object in the vicinity and say, "Try to pick that up." They always

207

pick it up. I say, "No, *try* to pick it up." They cannot 'try' to do the task. In the words of Yoda (Star Wars - The Empire Strikes Back), "Do. Or do not. There is no try." Using the word 'try' allows someone to avoid engaging and taking ownership of the task at hand. It allows them to renege or not complete a given task, seemingly with impunity. The damage that they do using the word 'try' is not measurable, but it is not an action word and does not foster trust. It does not help you to create a positive story about what you promise to accomplish. It gives the speaker a 'way out.' How often have you heard this from someone or even yourself, "Well, I tried." That is what is referred to as a copout. It results in non-action and reduced trust.

I encourage all my employees to speak in positive ways that open future possibilities, to be mindful of the power that they wield with their own language and their own self-talk. How they speak, the promises they make, and the follow-through that they generate help to create their futures, build trust, and generate a story of integrity about themselves. That is powerful.

Betty Eadie, a prominent American author, had this to say about the power of our language, "If we understood the power of our thoughts, we would guard them more closely. If we understood the awesome power of our words, we would prefer silence to almost anything negative. In our thoughts and words, we create our own weaknesses and our own strengths. Our limitations and joys begin in our hearts. We can always replace negative with positive."

Know that you have this power with language. Act and speak in a way that creates positivity for yourself and others around you. When you find yourself in difficult situations, reflect on the words you may have used that contributed to finding yourself there. Find words that will allow you to adjust the situation to a more positive one. Use your words to create the environment you want to function within.

When people ask me what I do, I often say that I 'manage mood' and 'help to invent reality.' It seems very esoteric and weird, does it not? I am in the hospitality industry, and mood is 90% of everything.

While mood can be created by the overall design and lighting, it is mostly set by the people who are working. Their mood is set by the owner, manager, or leader. It can also be set by external sources and strong personalities within the organization. It is the leader's job to create a space in which a positive mood of caring permeates. It is the leader's story about the work environment and their follow through on that story and their ability to actually live and act in it daily which creates this space of possibility. I say it creates the space since it is impossible to make everybody act in any certain way. However, it is possible to create the space in which everyone can feel free to act and behave however they chose to feel comfortable. I cannot make an employee behave the way I choose. I can, however, create a space and a mood through my words and actions that can have a positive influence on the employee and everyone else in the establishment. This practice has been tested scientifically [Scientific American – *The Me Effect* - Nicole Branan]. It is possible for every leader to build an environment of possibility if they prioritize and choose, in an effective way, to create a positive mood in the workplace.

Managing mood also helps to co-create the workplace reality. The existing reality of my workplace started its life as a thought. The thought became a story, and the story became action, and the action became a place of business. I was part of the process that created it. I co-created it with all the people who have self-selected to be a part of the business, to be a part of the story. I tell this story every day with my partners, managers, and employees. It is my job to maintain the story so that it is effective for all players. There are many aspects to my story and the reality the story creates. It includes the stories of other people as well. I cannot do this by myself, but I can point the story where I want it to go. Because I make the effort to continue telling that story, the story continues to generate the reality I envision. It is my job to create the 'common sense' for everyone in my story.

By managing mood and helping co-create reality, I have a fair amount of control over how any given day will go. I know that I do not really have control, it is more an influence, but I can control how

I react to situations that present themselves. If I act in a way that preserves and continues my story, I will be an effective leader. If I act in a way that is contrary to my story or betrays my concerns and the concerns of others, I will not be an effective leader. It is important to create the story, own the story, and act inside that story to generate positive moods and effective reality.

Tell Your Story

"If you do not design your own life plan, chances are you'll fall into someone else's plan. And guess what they have planned for you? Not much." - Jim Rohn

If you have not figured it out by now, this book is about you and the story that you get to tell with your thoughts, words, and actions. It is your narrative. Own that narrative and tell your own story. Own it and tell it to the best of your ability. Do not just be a minor character in other people's stories. Be the main character in your story. Be the person who acts, the person who takes care of others, all while taking care of yourself. When you take ownership of your story, you gain more control over the direction you go with your life. The caveat here is that we are also characters in other people's stories. In stories generated by groups of people, towns, cities, governments, etc., truth be told, there are some aspects of our lives over which we have little or no control. This is where acceptance comes in. It helps us shape our stories to focus on the aspects of our lives over which we have influence and a modicum of control.

Acceptance is an area where we can exert the most control in our daily lives. How we choose to react to external events in our lives goes a very long way toward creating more effective outcomes in our daily interactions. The first part of exercising control over your reactions is to learn to accept what is currently happening. Learning to accept and practicing acceptance is a vital first step on this path. Then you get to choose the most appropriate reaction for the given circumstances, and that correlates best to the future you are working to create.

Telling your story is vital to creating the future you want for yourself and those around you. From the time I dropped out of college, I always had a story about where I was going and what I wanted to accomplish when I got there. In my mid-thirties, I wrote out that story and worked to make it my reality. Dropping out of college set me on a path of learning whatever I could from the people around me who knew more than I did. I found that people liked to talk about what they do and were willing to teach me if I showed up eager to learn. The saying, "When the student is ready, the teacher will appear," often attributed to the Buddha, has certainly proven itself to be true for me in many cases.

When I moved to New Hampshire in the mid-eighties, it was my intent to become the head bartender at a nightclub that I liked and to land a job at a ski area that allowed me free skiing and the use of a snowmobile. I moved there at that time because my life in Boston was not allowing me enough time and money for skiing. So, I set out to fix that problem. By setting my intent, by creating that story, I was able to act in a way that helped me to manifest those jobs in my life. I became the head bartender in my second year, and by the end of the second ski season, I wrote a job description for a job that I saw was missing at the ski area. The job included skiing as part of the job and the use of a snowmobile. More importantly, the job description I wrote addressed a breakdown that the ski area had not fixed and effectively solved many longstanding problems within the lift department.

After working in that job for two years, I managed to reduce the number of injuries to lift attendants and skiers and reduce the downtime on lifts – while increasing customer satisfaction and employee retention. That year, the ski area ranked second in the nation for safety for mid-sized ski areas. By creating a position to take care of myself, I also created a position that worked incredibly well for the whole company. My story translated into improvements for everyone. **That is Selfish Altruism in action**.

By the way, when I was doing all that work at that time, I did not know what I know now. I just did what I thought was right. It is only in looking back with my current self that I can give words and a more meaningful story to the actions I engaged in at that time.

What is your story going to be? What do you want to manifest in your life? Take some time to think about how you want your life to turn out, in both the long-term and the short-term. I suggest writing it down. Engage in action that always supports your story. And, of course, do not engage in action that can betray that story.

If you want to be a manager in your department, start thinking about what actions you need to initiate to create that story. I have found that just by asking to learn more about what is required is a great place to start. If you can see what needs to be done, just start doing it. People want to work around people who can see the bigger picture and can act well inside of that story. Work in a way that helps to take care of others. Show up!

Your story is so important, and only you can create and tell it. Do not just be a minor character in someone else's story. Create a story where you are the person you want to be. Own your story.

Your People

"We have stopped for a moment to encounter each other, to meet, to love, to share. This is a precious moment, but it is transient. It is a little parenthesis in eternity. If we share with caring, lightheartedness, and love, we will create abundance and joy for each other. And then this moment will have been worthwhile."
- Deepak Chopra

You cannot do this alone. You arrive here via birth alone, and you will make the journey to death where you will be alone. Between, you need people to help you survive and to thrive. More importantly, you need the right people. It is through your words and actions that you build your friends, colleagues, and acquaintances. It is through engaging in trust and being trustworthy that you build relationships. It is through showing up as a committed and engaged person with a long-term story of care for yourself and those around you that you can create a meaningful life.

The people with whom we surround ourselves are the most significant influence on our behavior, attitudes, and results. With whom you spend time, what they have you thinking, saying, doing, and becoming will help to set the course of your life. In the words of motivational speaker, Jim Rohn, "You are the average of the five people you spend the most time with."

It has been said that the people with whom you habitually associate will determine as much as 95% of your success or failure in life. Through your journey, you will need people around you. The ideal way is to choose who those people are and be mindful of who they are not.

In his book *Works Well With Others*, author Ross McCammon has this to say about who we form relationships with. It is good advice:

Pick a person in your life — a friend, a co-worker, your cousin Kyle, whoever — and ask yourself two questions:

   1. Would I want to have two beers with this person?

   2. Would I trust them to look after my puppy over a weekend? You might have thought someone was "two beers and a puppy" and it turns out they're   "no beers and a puppy." (You do not really enjoy spending time with this person, but you think they're trustworthy.) Or maybe they are "two beers and no puppy." Sometimes people are "one beer and a puppy but only for, like, two hours on a Saturday." Some people are "limitless beers and an ocean of puppies." Some people are no on both counts. Your answers are guaranteed to be revealing. It might even lead you to seeing a relationship in a different way.

Creating Balance

"There's no such thing as work-life balance. There are work-life choices, and you make them, and they have consequences."
- Jack Welch

"Life is like riding a bicycle. To keep your balance, you must keep moving." - Albert Einstein

When I was in my teens and twenties, I am sure I did not think about balance unless I was attempting to walk after a few drinks. At that time, my life was about work, play, and sleep, pretty much in that order.

When I opened The Vanilla Bean Café with my family in 1989, I most certainly was not thinking about balance. We spent four months transforming a barn into a café and working long days to get it open. I was also bartending a few nights a week to earn enough money for gas and to make my car and insurance payments. I had some money for partying, but not much. I was also making time to see my girlfriend who lived two hours away.

Once we opened the restaurant, we all worked many long hours every day to make the place thrive and survive. I was working six days a week, 10 to 12 hours a day. Getting enough sleep was last on the list. There were days I only sat down for one meal.

Three years into the business, things began to settle down a bit. We had several employees and a few managers who helped to lighten the overall load, and we were all working more sensible hours and making a normal paycheck.

It was not until I got married that I started to think about balance, mostly at my wife's insistence. I realized that operating a restaurant was not conducive for a healthy family life and began to make changes toward a balance that would serve both the business and my family well.

There is a story in our culture that owning and running a restaurant is hard work and requires lots of long hours and that you cannot trust anyone to do it as well as you can. I decided that I did not agree with that story and set out to create a new one – one that took care of myself and my family, my business, and my employees, all while enhancing the overall customer experience. At that time, I was enrolled in a two-year business class based in California that helped me immensely to create this new and more balanced narrative. It was not easy, and it took years to create and embody this new story. It is still and always will be a work in progress because that is what life is for all of us (whether we realize it or not). It was also difficult because it was not in alignment with the cultural mindset about owning and operating restaurants.

Once I created the new narrative, both in writing and in my speaking, I set out to change the way I approach work and the way my business was structured. Some of the simple changes included a request that no managers or cooks could work over 45 hours a week (allowing for extenuating circumstances that could occasionally push it to 50). This also applied to me. Everyone could take two days off in a row if they chose to do so. Five personal days were added to the salaried manager's job descriptions. Most of the senior staff were cross-trained to be able to do every job in the place so that we could have easier coverage during difficult situations. I made the claim that if I could not accomplish my job duties in less than 40 hours a week, I had to make changes so that I could easily accomplish this. Many of these changes have been discussed in previous chapters. They include extending trust, educating, and empowering individual employees throughout the workforce, learning to make more effective requests and building more effective promisors. It became important to learn how to specify reality, i.e., create the 'common sense', and to manage the mood of the workplace. There are many parts to the narrative of restaurant operation. Over the years of creating, maintaining, and deepening the new story, I was able to grow a restaurant that defied the norm and take care of everyone in the process.

The narrative of long work hours is an old cultural artifact that is being challenged and changed by younger people in the workforce. Many of the younger people in today's workforce no longer want jobs that commit them to long hours and no balance. They do not see it as rewarding or fulfilling. They want jobs with shorter hours and the freedom to spend time on activities that keep them moving and engaged. "Millennials care more about work-life balance when choosing an employer (47%), while only 38% of Gen Z employees think it's important." (Vision Critical Research Company).

When I set out to write this chapter, I had a cultural mindset about what balance is for most of us in the United States. As I researched other people's interpretation of balance, I noticed that I did not have an adequate picture of what balance means in many people's lives. So, I took a few weeks off from writing to question as many people as I could, from different generations, about their interpretation of balance and whether they thought there was a shared cultural idea of what a balanced life looks like.

It is also important to note that I approach balance from my 20+ year practice of Tai Chi Chuan, in which I think about balance somatically and practice it almost daily. I also work to incorporate that concept of balance into my daily practices from walking, talking, and working to engaging with the world in various ways. (See *Tai Chi and the Practice of Business* in the Appendix).

In my discussions, I found that many people do think about their 'work-life balance.' A fairly new concept in our culture, it was first used in the United Kingdom and the United States in the late 1970s and 1980s. Work-life balance is commonly used to describe the balance between time that is allotted for work and time reserved for the other aspects of life. I find that people often 'struggle' to attain this balance, or they say that they have a hard time ' finding' this balance. Though some describe it as hard to find, others see this balance as a place of rest. Stephen Covey, the American educator, author, and businessman, had this to say about work-life balance: "The challenge of work-life balance is without question one of the most significant struggles faced by modern man."

Through my research, I learned about two kinds of balance in scientific discourse: static balance and dynamic balance. Static balance refers to the ability of a stationary object to balance. It happens when the object's center of gravity is on the axis of rotation. On the other hand, dynamic balance is the ability of an object to balance while in motion or switching between positions. I tend to think that, in humans, we are almost always talking about dynamic balance. That is because it refers to the ability to balance while in motion or to switch between positions. This definition of dynamic balance can be applied not only to our physical bodies but also to our stories of 'work-life balance 'and to our daily actions that help us to take care of our concerns. Everything is always in motion. When I think of static balance, I think of stasis or of something that is inert and not a living system. While balancing on one leg, it may look like static balance, but "there are many systems interacting and coordinating in precise and complex ways" (Peter M. Wayne, Ph. D.) for us to maintain that balance. So that relative stillness is not static balance.

In exploring the systems that help us to keep balanced, we find that there are four body systems that must work together to keep us from falling: musculoskeletal, sensory, neuromuscular, and cognitive. Working to keep balance in our lives will also require skill with our linguistic self, the language we use to tell our story. How does the story we tell ourselves about concerns compare to the practices we engage to fulfill those concerns? It is the overlap of those two spheres that helps us to achieve balance and produce meaning in our lives. The diagram below illustrates how a concern for staying healthy – by getting enough exercise and sleep and by eating well – helps to create balance.

Needless to say, if weight loss is a concern related to achieving your life-balance, then the practices of drinking sugary sodas and eating greasy foods will not get you there.

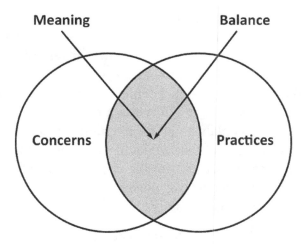

Figure 9 – Balance Diagram

I have come to believe that many people think about balance the wrong way. They speak and act as if balance is a place of harmony and stasis. To me, balance is a place of challenge and action. Think of riding a bicycle; to achieve balance while riding, it is much easier to do so while you are in motion. Remaining stationary on a bicycle is much more difficult and requires a great deal more effort and a great deal more attention. While riding a bicycle can be enjoyable at times (downhill) and difficult at other times (uphill), it is being in motion that makes it easier, uphill or down, to maintain balance. Thinking in this way, we can see that achieving balance requires us to be in motion because we are a living system. This is dynamic balance. The reason people struggle to find balance is because, just like riding a bicycle, they are not sufficiently engaged in purposeful action to achieve balance. Because they may find it difficult to engage in such action, they 'struggle' to find balance. The reason some people cannot find balance is that it is not a 'thing' to be 'found,',' as though balance was a place of arrival and stasis. Rather it is action-related, and we 'find' it only when we are engaged in it and engaged with purposeful action. I think of the cliché about life being the journey and not the destination. Balance is the action, not the result.

By working with balance, we produce results like time with family and friends, time at meaningful work, time for ourselves, etc. By thinking about balance in this way, we can remove the negative words that tend to cluster around the concept, like *struggle* and *difficult.* We can recognize that achieving balance involves motion and work. Just like engaging in riding a bicycle or engaging in any sport, we do not complain about the exertion because it is part of the sport. By understanding that achieving balance involves exertion, we can then come to terms with the notion of 'work-life balance ' and enjoy the results that we create as we engage in producing balance and meaning in our story.

One of my friends had this to say when I asked her about balance (the italics are mine):

"Balance in life means that you are calm, centered, and clear in your mind, body, and spirit. If you are balanced, you feel calm in your body. You take time to meditate and relax. You are able to shut off your [monkey] brain and be present in your life at any given moment. Balance is all about how present you can be and how in alignment you are with who you see yourself to be and what your purpose is on the planet. *I think it is much easier to find balance and flow state when you are doing what you are meant to be doing.* We tend to get out of alignment when our thoughts/emotions/actions do not line up with what our higher self wants us to do on the planet."
- Natalie Susi, USCD Professor, and entrepreneur.

Balance appears when we are in action and doing meaningful work. It will be hard at times; it will be easy at times. Just ask a tightrope walker what it takes to balance.

Through any given day, week, or stretch of your life, you may feel unbalanced. That is just incredibly normal. Getting yourself back to a balanced state takes practice. Getting back to a balanced state can take years of work. Master Morihei Ueshiba, the founder of the martial art Aikido, stood less than five feet tall and weighed well under 100 pounds. Yet he could remain centered, calm, and apparently stable, even while evading the attack of multiple opponents. He was fond of telling his students that he was not as stable and balanced as they perceived, "It is not that I stay balanced all the time. I just recover so fast; nobody notices the imbalances." I often refer to martial arts as a way to see your somatic self in motion. You can also look at your linguistic self the same way. There are many times in a day that you will be knocked off balance; you will forget what you care about and act in ways that betray your long-term story of care. But just like practicing a martial art to establish or recover balance, you can practice your own linguistic art. This art means taking care of your own story through being mindful of your actions and creating a practice to recover so fast that no one notices that you lost your balance.

By working with this interpretation of balance, I find that I create more peace in all aspects of my life. By accepting that balance is my work, I find my workdays have become easier to navigate. I am also in a better place to help others accomplish their work in a more effective and well-balanced way.

Food

"People who love to eat are always the best people." - *Julia Child*

"First we eat, then we do everything else." - *M.F.K. Fisher*

What would a book about working in the hospitality industry be without a least one chapter on food? Food is an important part of our everyday lives, and often you will find that community is built around food and food rituals from growing, preparing, and consuming that which gives us life in more ways than one.

I learned to cook long before I opened a restaurant, but operating a restaurant certainly helped me to deepen my knowledge about food. I learned to cook partly because both my mother and father were good cooks and because I like to eat good food. I like to see, taste, touch, smell, and feel good food. It excites all my senses. Often was the time when we would go out to eat, and we would leave saying that mom could have made it better at home, and she always did. As kids, we could choose to go out to a restaurant of our choice for our birthday or have mom make our favorite dish at home. I always asked for baked stuffed shrimp and lemon meringue pie – made by Mom. Who needs cake?

If you care about food and care about what you eat, learn to cook, or make friends with people who love to cook. Well, you could do that, but you really should learn to cook. These days, you can find easy and short recipes online or on YouTube; follow enough of those, and you can learn very quickly. If you purchase a cookbook, buy one with pictures. That way, you know that someone followed the recipe, and it worked. I have recently watched Jacques Pepin and his short videos on making a quick delicious meal with food items you probably have on hand or are easily acquired. He presents in such a way that is easy to follow and easy to do.

I like to buy cookbooks with the history of the recipes, as this deepens my knowledge of cooking in general and helps me when I write my own recipes. I like to know what spices and seasonings are used culturally and regionally and how they are used. When I want to write a new recipe, I will look up many recipes for the same dish. I will look up the cultural history of the same dish and other spices that are used in that region. I will then write the new recipe based on my new knowledge, my own understanding, and my own methods.

Most importantly, expand you own palate. We often limit our choices to what we know because of where we grew up or is popular and prevalent in the marketplace in which we live. The world is literally full of things to eat. There is a vast array of cultural cuisines from around the world from which to partake and sample. Do not limit yourself because of your current food prejudices. Keep in mind that prejudice implies the holding of an opinion or the making of a judgment without sufficient knowledge. Few of us like to admit to having prejudices of any kind because it implies irrational thinking and not having an open mind. Calvin W. Schwabe has this to say about food prejudices in his book *Unmentionable Cuisine*, "Food dislikes are not prejudices if they are based upon a sufficient range of experiences and a willingness to recognize that tastes may change or palates may be educated." So, keep trying new foods when at all possible, expand your own palate and your own food knowledge. It has the potential to make you a hit at parties.

Our likes and dislikes of certain foods can have many causes, and our own brain can trick us into not liking something that we may have happily consumed before. It turns out that these food aversions can be challenged if you are willing. For example, I do not like goat cheese, but I keep trying goat cheese. Occasionally I find one that I like. I am still not a fan, but it does not stop me from trying a new one if it crosses my path.

I grew up in a household where we, as children, were expected to try anything new in the way of food that showed up on the table. It was not always easy, but it helped me to be an exploratory eater in my late teens and early twenties when there were not many people straying too far from what they already consumed.

At the restaurants, we ask all our employees to be open-minded about the food we offer and to willingly try something new or even something to which they might have an aversion. Some people find that they like foods they thought they did not like. Others find out that they still do not like a certain food, but as an ingredient in a dish, they find that they like that food. One example of this is when I had an employee who would not try our gazpacho soup because she did not like tomatoes. A very valid reason, but she had never tried gazpacho. At some urging, she eventually tried our gazpacho. She loved it. As years passed, she would stop in occasionally to let me know that she always tries gazpacho when it is on a menu somewhere, but 'ours' was still the best. She still does not like tomatoes.

Speaking of tomatoes, my own daughter does not like tomatoes either. Recently, I made a bruschetta with local heirloom tomatoes and served it on fresh, locally made ciabatta that had been toasted with herbed olive oil. She loved it. She asked me to make it again, and we had it again a few days later. I must agree with her about tomatoes that are available year-round in the grocery store. They are mostly like red cardboard. I fully understand her dislike. A fresh heirloom tomato is a different thing altogether. Made into a fresh bruschetta on fresh bread, it is almost heavenly. You will find a recipe for that bruschetta at the end of this chapter. It is best to make this in late July, August, or early September when heirloom tomatoes can be found at your local farmer's market. While you are there, get as many of the ingredients for this recipe you can find.

Do not avoid specific ingredients because you do not like them. You will find that all the ingredients are in a dish for a reason. Most recipes are working to create a balanced flavor, and removing one item can throw off the whole dish. Good cooking and great meals are all about balance, and recipes have been created and tested to create this balance. Samin Nosrat, the author of *Salt, Fat, Acid, Heat: Mastering the Elements of Good Cooking,* has this to say about creating balance, "Season food with the proper amount of salt at the proper moment; choose the optimal medium of fat to convey the flavor of your ingredients; balance and animate those ingredients with acid; apply the right type and quantity of heat for the proper amount of time—do all this and you will turn out vibrant and beautiful food, with or without a recipe." Balance in a recipe is so important.

I know bartenders who will not use a certain type of alcohol or mixer in a drink because they do not like it. Mixed drinks are created the same way a good food dish is created; a variety of flavor agents are mixed, and a balance of flavors is created. Omit one ingredient, and the drink will be unbalanced and not be as good as it could be. A simple way to look at this is with one of the most used flavoring agents in the United States food world, pepper. Lots of people use pepper in their cooking, and many dishes would not be the same without it. But you would not eat pepper on its own. You would not like it. This same reasoning holds true for most other ingredients. They are there for a reason, and to omit them changes the balance of the food or drink and does both the recipe and you a disservice, not to mention the people you are serving.

Working in a restaurant, you just learn more about food. Working in an independent, chef-driven restaurant, you learn a lot about food. It comes with the territory. Unlike working for the undertaker, it adds a lot more spice to your life. If you work at a restaurant, learn as much as you can about food and its preparation. If you have any other job, get a few good cookbooks, look up recipes on the internet, watch YouTube demonstrations, anything to help you expand your knowledge and your ability in the kitchen.

Seriously, if you do not know how to cook, learn to cook. Meaningful friendships are created in the kitchen and around the dinner table. Eating is necessary for survival, so you might as well make the most of it, enjoy every step of the process, and every bite along the way. As American chef and food writer, Ruth Reichl, puts it, "Pull up a chair. Take a taste. Come join us. Life is so endlessly delicious."

Bruschetta Recipe

1/4 cup extra virgin olive oil
4 cloves minced fresh garlic
2 cups heirloom tomatoes, diced
1/4 cup chopped fresh basil
1 tablespoon balsamic vinegar
1/2 teaspoon sea salt - more to taste
1/4 teaspoon freshly ground black pepper
1 loaf of fresh ciabatta
1/4 cup finely shredded fresh parmesan
    cheese

1. Heat olive oil in a small frypan over medium-low heat. Add garlic and sauté until just starting to turn golden (do not brown it). Add to mixing bowl to cool

2. Chop tomatoes and basil and add to mixing bowl

3. Add balsamic vinegar, salt and pepper, and mix well

4. Slice the bread, rub with olive oil, and sprinkle lightly with sea salt

5. Toast in the oven on a sheet pan until golden brown

To serve, top the bread slices with the bruschetta mixture and sprinkle with parmesan.

Think Like an Entrepreneur

"The greatest discovery of our generation is that human beings can alter their lives by altering their attitudes of mind. As you think, so shall you be." - William James

Entrepreneurial thinking is the ability to see things differently than most other people. It is not necessarily a trait that is inherent; people can work to develop this type of thinking and, for those who have it, it can be improved upon. Entrepreneurial thinking allows you to see differently and be exposed to new learning opportunities that can help you create for yourself new, more exciting roles in your future. Some people seem to have the ability from a young age to see new possibilities and drifts in the marketplace and how they can be monetized. Many people learn this way of seeing the world through their education and life choices. Sometimes we learn from other people through planned or chance meetings or through acquaintances.

To be an entrepreneur and to practice entrepreneurial thinking are two different things. Many people in workplaces are not entrepreneurs in the traditional sense but practice entrepreneurial thinking regularly. I am suggesting that you do not have to strike out on your own to adopt some of the traits of an entrepreneurial mindset.

Throughout this book, I have offered a different way to see and interact with the world and the marketplace. This different way is a form of entrepreneurial thinking. My intention is that you may adopt ideas and practices mentioned in this book that resonate with you and then work to establish a different way of seeing and interacting with your reality. Work on them one at a time. Come back to sections where you want to deepen your own narrative. Use the internet to seek out more information on how entrepreneurs see the world.

Thinking with an entrepreneurial mindset is how people work to create and co-create our world space. It is a practice that can be cultivated just like any practice. Just like any practice, it will be natural for some, while others will struggle to get there. Like anything in life, some people will excel, and others will move onto something else. If you stick with the notion that we all have the power to create, then it may be possible that we all have the ability for entrepreneurial thinking. Many people are just not exposed to it in such a way that it can become a possibility for them.

Some people can make a living as an entrepreneur, while others find that path to be too unpredictable. You do not have to make a living being an entrepreneur to begin thinking like one. Many companies have entrepreneurial thinkers on their staffs. Many of those companies could not compete in the marketplace if they did not have those employees.

Our culture equates owning a business with being an entrepreneur; this is often not the case. Being an entrepreneur means engaging in different thinking and in new and more effective business practices, as well as taking calculated risks. On the other hand, many business owners have just created a company by mimicking others in the marketplace. True entrepreneurs change the marketplace and/or are able to create new offers in the marketplace. The main thing is to keep on learning and making the attempt to see the world not as a fixed and knowable place but as a place always in flux where there are always openings and closings in the marketplace.

Have Fun! – Learn Things!

"The more that you read, the more things you will know. The more that you learn, the more places you'll go." - Dr. Seuss

"It is fun to have fun, but you have to know how." - Dr. Seuss

Have Fun! – Learn Things! This has been my mantra from my teens to my present. When I dropped out of college, I decided that I needed to learn from as many people as I could, whether I encountered them in my travels or my places of work. I also wanted to have Fun because engaging in fun activities is also a way of learning. It is a well-established fact that children learn through play. So, it stands to reason that, even as adults, we can continue in that vein.

Throughout my working career, I have always made it a point to put Fun in the work that I had to do. I would often find ways, like learning to juggle and dressing up as a clown, to create a Fun environment and some lasting memories.

Creating a sense of play in the workday helps to relieve stress and makes it easier to engage with co-workers and customers. I was hired as a bartender for a Christmas Party for a local company that created unique dolls that had a very specific look. When I bartended for their holiday party, I dressed up and applied makeup to look like one of their dolls. It was Fun for me, as well as for many of my fellow employees. My co-bartender also had Fun making Fun of me all night. It was one of my best tip nights for a private party ever.

When you are in a good mood, it is also much easier to engage in learning new things. It just happens naturally. Humans are natural learners, and when we stir a sense of Fun into the learning process, we automatically resort to our natural way of being, and we learn better.

Love It!

"Love is the grounding of our existence as humans and is the basic emotioning in our systemic identity as human beings."
- Humberto Maturana – The Tree of Knowledge

"Love does not dominate; it cultivates."
- Johann Wolfgang von Goethe

In the hospitality business, it is obvious that we are here to help take care of others. We are in it because we love the work that we do. We love making a difference in other people's lives. We are here for the customers and love forming deeper relationships with them. We are also in it to care for all who enter our establishment, from the dishwasher to the last customer to leave. We are in the hospitality business from a sense of love. People stay in the hospitality business because they love their job.

We are told by life coaches to follow our passion. Do what you love, and money will follow. While this can be good advice, it is not always easy to execute. You can, however, work from a place of passion within the work where you find yourself. The reason is easy. Each moment of now is about you. Why not engage in a way that helps to generate passion? In every job I have had, I have worked to find a way to love the job. If I did not love the job out of the gate, I worked to make changes so that it could become a job that I loved. If I could not make it a job I loved, I left it to find one I could love. I worked to have people around for me whom I could care and with whom I loved spending time on a regular basis.

I tell my managers that when it comes down to taking care of the staff, you really must love them. You must come from a place of genuine care. When you can do that, you are able to create a team of people who love each other. When you have a team like that, hospitality happens as a natural consequence. A positive working environment will just happen if it is fostered from a place of genuine hospitality, love, and care. There is no effort in creating it. From my 20-plus years of practicing Tai Chi, this is what is referred to as effortless power. Our managers do what they can to take care of our employees in their jobs and, where appropriate, in their outside lives too. We all work together to take care of the customers and the concerns that they have. We do this with a sense of purpose and a sense of care. Developing a place of hospitality starts with approaching it with a sense of passion and then being welcoming to the staff and everyone else involved. It also includes being hospitable to your vendors, delivery personnel, and other people we encounter in our daily practice of business.

At one of our restaurants, we take such good care of our main supplier's driver that he purchased Christmas presents for our receiving staff. When staff takes good care of our delivery drivers, they, in turn, take good care of our staff, and in doing so, takes care of our business.

The cool thing about love is that when you compare it to something static like, say, a pencil, then you can see how its effect is exponential. If I have a pencil and I give it to someone, they have a pencil, and I do not. If I have knowledge and I give it to someone, then it is shared knowledge. Love takes it a step further. True, if I give someone love, then they have love, and I also still have love, but if they choose to give it back to me, I now have more love than when I started. Not only that, but they can give this love to others, and it becomes more powerful every time it is given. This exponential growth makes love a force in this world that can have a large and lasting impact. If we care to look, we can see this in action every day. However, it does not make good 'news,' so it is not shown to us every day by the media.

If we can operate from a sense of shared love in our businesses, our lives, and for ourselves, then it makes functioning in and living this life better for everyone involved. Taking the notion of Selfish Altruism to heart, we care for ourselves so that we can care for others, we love ourselves so that we can love others, and we love and care for ourselves *when* we love and care for others. By living into this quality of Selfish Altruism, we can work to create a more caring and loving world around us, all with the true sense of hospitality.

According to Brené Brown, American professor, lecturer, and author, "shame, blame, disrespect, betrayal and the withholding of affection damage the roots from which love grows." That means that any one of these actions in a workplace will work against creating a caring and loving environment. This, of course, is also true in all relationships.

Keep in mind that "love includes trust, respect, kindness, and affection" (Brené Brown). We must operate in all these domains to create a loving environment. This also holds true for how we treat ourselves. We must cultivate these domains in and for ourselves. Then we can cultivate them in the external world in a much more meaningful and effortless way.

One of our restaurants, Dog Lane Café, is such a loving place that it is a life-changing event for many of the young people who choose to work there with us. The staff really cares about their co-workers, which makes the whole day a much more enjoyable experience for all involved. It also matters when people need some extra help or a shift covered; there are many people who will step up to help. We have customers who come in and sit in such a way that they can observe our staff at play. For people who are good observers of everyday life, the way Dog Lane Café functions is an anomaly (Last year, the 'Love' food modifier in the register system was used 43,154 times and 'Thank You' was used 37,500 times – for contrast, the word 'No' was used 11,895 times). Our customers love to be a part of the energy that is created because of the love that is practiced. While all our restaurants have this to some degree, Dog Lane Café was designed so that all employees can see the customers, and so that all customers can see the employees if they so choose. Our other restaurants have a smaller portion of the staff visible at any given time, and some of the staff cannot be seen at all. It is harder to create a team of people who do not function closely with each other every day if they cannot see each other.

We have found that when the entire staff can see the customers, there is a better connection and hence better energy between the staff and the customers.

If you are someone in charge of the hiring, it is important to bring in people that will fit well with the culture you want to create. It is equally as important to remove the people that are not a fit. I tell all of our partners and managers in charge of hiring to only hire people that they genuinely like. We seek people who are friendly, kind, and loving. We can teach these people almost anything. Conversely, we have found it very difficult to teach someone who presents as not having a friendly, kind, and loving manner.

I also tell our hiring managers and partners to get rid of people they are not genuinely happy to see every day. If they have an employee who makes them groan or sends them into avoid mode, it is time to get rid of that employee. Of course, the manager or partner needs to be aware of their own issues at that moment to prevent them from treating the employee unfairly. This is not about one-offs; this is about someone who is constantly not a fit for the organization. It is a disservice to us to keep people around who are not people our co-workers want to see every day. It is also a disservice to the employee, who likely feels some of the same vibes and is therefore not happy about being there. This is love at work, tough as it may seem, and will help to keep the place functioning from a place of genuine care. As I said above, when love is happening, hospitality is just a natural consequence.

Work to create the place where you want to be every day. Work to create the same space for your employees. If you love what you are doing, the right people will show up to help further your sense of love. That, in turn, will attract the right customers. You want everyone to say, "I love that place!"

This works at home too! I was fortunate enough to have parents that were truly loving and hospitable people. Most likely why I found my career in the hospitality industry, it is a place I truly love.

Figure 10 – Drunkard's Path Heart Stitch

Live It!

"The purpose of life, after all, is to live it, to taste experience to the utmost, to reach out eagerly and without fear for newer and richer experience." - *Eleanor Roosevelt*

Did you know that there are sharks that must keep moving forward, or they will not get enough oxygen passing over their gills, and they will die? There are about two dozen species, including the great white, the whale shark, and the mako shark, that are known as "obligate ram ventilators," meaning it is quite essential for them to keep moving to stay alive. It is actually easier for these particular species of sharks to keep moving than to stay still. Even these sharks can catch a break every once in a while and rest up for a moment before swimming off again. The point of sharing this is to remind you just to keep moving forward. Or, as Dory in *Finding Nemo* is fond of saying, "Just keep swimming."

Out of all the information I have shared in this book, there are three pieces that have been vital for many of my successes and without which I could not be doing what I do, nor could I have created what I now surround myself with day in and day out.

The first piece of information is that 'I work for myself.' I knew at an early age that by adopting the mindset of working for myself and the future that I was creating, I would be able to work to the best of my abilities. When I first adopted this mindset, I cannot pinpoint. It may have been that the first job I had ended up being owned by the bank. It may just have been innate to me from the beginning. Many of my co-workers throughout my early career have said to me, "Barry, you should own your own place." They said this because they observed that I functioned from a place of deep care that many of my co-workers did not possess. I had this level of care because I was working for myself and not the owners or managers. At the same time, I was working for the customers because I knew that is from where the money comes. I got hit by a strong wave of satisfaction whenever I could make the day a little brighter for a customer or a co-worker. I loved functioning in such a way that I made the work more fun and much easier for many of my co-workers. From this 'place' that I created for myself, I learned all that I have learned and gained the knowledge that I have gained. It also allowed me to build a reputation that helped open possibilities for me, including raises, promotions, and new jobs, oh, and restaurants!

The second piece of knowledge that has allowed me to be more effective in all I have chosen to do is realizing that as humans, we live in language. As I have mentioned previously, I was exposed to this understanding from a business class I took in the late 1990s in California. We create all that we do because of our use of language. Knowing this and using language as a tool – concisely – has allowed me to create an effective future. By using language to specify what I care about and launching effective practices, I have learned that I have taken care of so many of my life concerns.

The third practice I find vital for my life is to engage every day from a place of Selfish Altruism. I want to create a better life for myself, but I also take great joy in helping others to do the same. In my mind, it helps to create a better and more satisfying life and future.

Using language as a tool for the power of creation has allowed me to be a designer of many aspects of my life. It has allowed me to design offers in the marketplace, design workspaces, and even design conversations of care. With language, I am essentially an artist. We all are.

You are an artist. You get to create with language. You get to specify the direction your life will take, but you must step up and own it. You can no longer allow your language to label you as a victim. You can no longer allow negative talk in your conversations or your own self-talk. Fire your inner critic and hire an inner coach! With mindful practice, you will be able to use your language, your words to create a world space around you that helps you to effectively take care of what it is that you *say* you care about.

For optimists, this will be easier, as they are already using positive language to see the world. For the pessimists, it will be a little harder. It starts with framing what we see in each moment from a place of good, a place of potential for good. By 'good', I mean to see it in a way that supports your story and the story of others with which you surround yourself. From there, it requires engaging in the effective use of language to mobilize yourself and others around you to create the world space you want to live and thrive within.

Using the tools and ideas in this book (and from other books and conversations as well), you have the potential to be much more effective than if you just go through life with a fatalistic attitude. You must remember that there are many more forces at play in this world space, and you may not always end up where you intended. In theory, you will still be better off than if you had done nothing to take ownership for the direction of your life and for taking care of the lives of those people in this life that you care about.

The world is not a static place. Change is always the name of the game. Be a part of the change, or as this quotation often attributed to Mahatma Gandhi, Indian lawyer, and political ethicist, clearly states, "Be the change you want to see in the world."

By the way, this is the real quotation:
"We but mirror the world. All the tendencies present in the outer world are to be found in the world of our body. If we could change ourselves, the tendencies in the world would also change. As a man changes his own nature, so does the attitude of the world change towards him. This is the divine mystery supreme. A wonderful thing it is and the source of our happiness. We need not wait to see what others do." – Mahatma Gandhi

Your words have power. Use that power wisely.

So, that is it. That is all I have for now. I know I will have more later because I am still a beginner in many areas. I am still learning, I am still creating, and I am still having Fun. How about you?

The Last Page

It looks like you made it to The Last Page.

It looks like you made it to the 'End.'

It may seem to you like the 'End.'

It is not.

It may seem like you 'Finished.'

You did not.

You may want The Last Page to tie all the previous pages together. You know, The Last Page is where all those previous words are to merge into one meaningful sentence. One meaningful 'takeaway.'

All those previous pages just contain thoughts and ideas.

They contain Stories.

They are only meaningful if you found meaning in them.

Likely you did find some new meaning. Certainly not on every page.

Perhaps there were some nuggets of wisdom that you can use.

To take and practice. To make your own.

But The Last Page is also supposed to help. So you say.

Perhaps point in a meaningful direction.

Because you are looking for it, I will point out such a direction:

You. And the story you will create. That will create you.

Your Narrative.

This is really a new First Page.

It is blank.

Your future is waiting.

Begin your story – embrace your Narrative.

Set your intent.

Surround yourself with caring people.

Learn things.

Have Fun!

(Ok, so it is not really the last page; there is also the appendix and the legal stuff, so there is a little more reading to do. Be sure to see the real last page).

Appendix

"The key to a great life lies in shifting your focus from accumulation to contribution. The old saying "He who gathers the most toys wins" needs to be replaced with "He who serves the most prospers". Remember, happiness is the by-product of a life spent adding value to other people's lives."

- Robin Sharma

AFFIRM - Problem Solving for Difficult Situations

AFFIRM: *Accept, Forgive, Focus, Investigate, Resolve, Move On*

This acronym refers to steps that you can take to help you resolve problems or difficult situations in your life. I started working on pieces of this practice for myself after I was exposed to the Buddhist concept of acceptance and forgiveness. Truthfully, I started working on it in my teens when I discovered that certain feelings and the reaction generated by them were almost always self-sabotaging. It took about 15 more years to really go deeper into the Buddhist concepts to find a way to develop a way of being that included these concepts. I learned that acceptance is being open to the actual feelings we are having in every moment as we experience them and being willing to sit with and experience those feelings without judgment or reaction. Buddhism teaches the importance of acceptance and forgiveness are critical steps to achieving a peaceful state of mind as well as a peaceful way of life. Believe me, approaching running restaurants from this state of mind is much easier to do than the common sense that it is a stressful environment.

I continued to expand on acceptance and forgiveness to be able to move on from a situation. That is how this acronym came into being. One day I was talking to a customer (I do that a lot) who was sitting alone, and we ended up on the philosophical side of things in our discussion. It turns out that this customer was a priest from a local church, and we were talking about the power of forgiveness. I decided to tell him about the practice that I had been developing and teaching to my senior managers. I went into the acronym listed above and covered the whole thing. He said to me, "You need to write that down." So, I did. This is it.

We all have times when situations appear to be out of our control, and our reactions to them can create bigger problems. It is important to initiate internal change in such a way that it does not exacerbate the external problem. Part of the problem is that we thought the situations were in our control in the first place. Giving up the idea of control helps to mitigate problems and, more importantly, your reactions to them. We all operate under the idea that we have some control over external events. We do not. We can have immense impact on how situations develop based on our own intent, actions, and resolve, but all kinds of unforeseen things can go wrong. Once you give up control and begin expecting things to go wrong, you are on a path to a more peaceful day, week, month, life.

It is our reactions to problems and situations that often make them worse. By following the steps outlined below, you will find that where you do have control is over how you react to the situations. That is power.

The first two steps are the hardest for most people who have grown up in our culture of blame. Once you get by those two steps, you will find that the next four are accomplished much easier. So, let us take a look at the steps. I will then go into detail about each one:

Accept what is happening or has happened.

Forgive yourself and all participants so that you do not act out of anger (or any other damaging mood).

Focus yourself and your energy on the situation with intent to create a more effective outcome.

Investigate (1) what caused the breakdown(s), (2) your motivations for effective change, and (3) your resources for making change.

Resolve to make changes and corrections that will help to

Move On. No regrets; no what-ifs; no coulda-woulda-shouldas. Look back only for lessons while engaging in the process again.

A problem is presenting in your world space that is causing you to be upset in the present moment. The first thing to do is to fully **Accept** the problem at hand (really, the first thing to do is not blame someone else). Wishing it was not happening is counterproductive or resorting to 'if only' in such a way that renders you powerless. "If only I had …," is the start of a conversation with no power. You have this moment alone and the resources around you for moving forward. 'What-ifs 'just paralyze you in the present moment and render you a victim. Fully accepting the present situation allows you to move to the next step.

The ability to **Forgive** is something with which many people struggle. There have been many things written about this ability. From my perspective, when you cannot forgive, you only damage yourself. Being angry at someone is like taking a poison and expecting the other person to die. Not forgiving is self-harm. Not forgiving yourself is also self-harm. Holding grudges and being angry does absolutely nothing to solve any given problem. Look at all the times you have been unforgiving or angry toward someone, and you will see that nothing good ever came of those situations. If you still think that it is justifiable, you are being delusional. If you must be angry, be angry and take care of it as peaceably as possible. If you hold on to anger and refuse to forgive, you are hurting only yourself on many levels. Angry people tend to get more diseases. Dis-ease. Think about that.

Engaging in forgiveness for yourself and others is not easy and is a practice to develop. It takes time to break old habits and ways of being. Mindfulness is the first step in creating this practice. It is not magic, and it takes time. Once you can forgive in the moment, you will find it is much easier to move forward and find peace.

When you are at peace, you will be able to **Focus** your attention on the situation at hand. When you are thinking clearly, you can better understand the situation from many sides and not just from your immediate perspective. You can see what may have caused the problem and may be able to see a clearer path to change the situation. You will be in a much better place to **Investigate** the situation and the players involved.

The investigation process includes the actions leading up to the situation, the actual situation itself, and the resources at hand to work to create a more favorable outcome. The investigation also involves an exploration of yourself and what triggers you. Sometimes doing nothing is the best plan of attack; more will be revealed as time passes. The need to do something right away is part of our culture of getting things done. You do not have to do that. Sometimes the investigation process will reveal that waiting is the best course of action. You may need to work on not being reactionary in the heat of the situation. The main point of the investigation process is to discover your internal triggers and learn from this exploration what YOU can do differently, both in the moment and in the future. This puts you in a more effective place to reach a resolution.

An effective **Resolve** will fix the immediate problem; it may also help to mitigate any future problems. The Resolve may use the resources you have on hand, or it may require resources you will have to acquire. Either way, the aim of any proposed Resolve is to change the current unsatisfactory situation to a satisfactory one. It may work well, it may not. With continued practice, you will get more effective and be able to approach the Resolve with a sense of peace.

Once the situation has been changed to a more favorable one, it is important to **Move-on**. Do not get caught up in second guessing or replaying the problem over and over. Eventually a similar problem will present itself, and then you may review the past Resolve but not to get to a different outcome for the old problem. This time the emphasis for your Resolve will be on deeper learning and/or teaching for fixing the new problem. Again – all you have is the present moment and where that is headed. Going back with a list of 'what-ifs 'or refusing to declare 'lesson learned' is useless, a waste of your time, energy, and resources.

The next time you find yourself in a difficult situation or faced with a problem, take the time to **AFFIRM**. Engage a process that creates a more successful outcome and effective resolution and, at the same time, a more peaceful you. I must reiterate here that this is not magic. It takes a lot of work to function in the present moment. It takes not only self-reflection and a hard look at ourselves and how we see the world but also an honest critique of how we act in each moment based on our own biases. The more you take time to work on yourself and become a more effective you, the more adept you become at taking care of problems or difficult situations in the present moment.

Traits to Embody to Create a More Valuable You

You have probably all seen a list of 10 traits that require zero talent that is often shared on the internet and social media sites. This statement about requiring zero talent is far from the truth. The word *trait* is used as if it were referring to an innate talent, one with which you were born and not one that has been cultivated and practiced over time. It also completely diminishes the work that people have done to acquire these traits. I have worked with hundreds of people, and I have seen firsthand how the top people work at being the top people. They work to embody practices that help them take care of themselves and allow them to take care of others. They are *Selfishly Altruistic* in their actions. They embody the traits they have because they have worked at building them to the point that they have become skills. The 'top people' have a sense of care for themselves and others. They have spent the time and attention to strengthening the traits that have made them an effective employee, team member, supervisor, manager, owner – and a more valuable self.

These are traits you need to practice and the skills you need to embody to be an effective member of any team while working toward becoming an effective leader (and a more valuable you in the future):

1. Arrive early
2. Be in a good mood
3. Say 'yes' to requests in a mood of willingness
4. Interact positively with co-workers and customers
5. Be helpful
6. Be reliable – cultivate trust
7. Be willing to learn – anything
8. Take on the difficult jobs/tasks
9. Be prepared

10. Engage each day with a sense of Fun
11. Ask for help when you need it
12. Easily admit mistakes
13. Do not play the blame game
14. Be coachable
15. Do not complain – offer solutions
16. Be self-motivated (mobilized)
17. Effectively communicate ideas
18. Show leadership qualities
19. Engage with honesty and integrity
20. Cultivate a sense of passion

It is through awareness and practice that we develop our talents so that they become embodied skills. Develop the first 10 skills on this list, and you will become a top employee. Then develop the second 10 on this list, and you will be preparing to become an effective leader.

Work on them one at a time. Be mindful of which trait you are practicing until it becomes ingrained as a way of being. If you have developed a number of these traits already, work on the one that you have been avoiding. Learn and practice these skills, and you will find that the world of work opens for you. Employers want to surround themselves with people who embody and value these traits.

I often tell people that it is easy to succeed; all you must do is just be better than everyone else, and that is not hard. Most people are not aware of the need for these traits and that they must be practiced effectively. They do not attempt to do the work to build these skills. So, put in the effort to develop even the first four on the list, and you are on your way to being better than most. Post the first 10 in your room or office where you will see them every day.

All the traits listed above are fundamentally promises that you make to yourself and to those around you. A great employer will help you to develop and manage these promises. When an employer or manager makes requests of you, you will be someone who can fulfill those requests. You will be assessed as a reliable employee, a good promisor, and someone everyone will want on their team. Embodying this knowledge will also open other possibilities throughout your career. Be the person with which everyone wants to work. Learn and develop these traits until they become embodied skills. When practiced regularly, they all add up to what we call good working habits or work ethics. When you do the work to embody these traits, you will find that the effort you invest will help to create a more valuable YOU in your future.

What Does It Take?

A great restaurant creates an illusion for the average customer that running a restaurant can be all very easy. This may be one of the reasons so many people want to open restaurants. They believe that they can easily achieve what a great restaurant does consistently and recurrently through years of practice. I have noticed that the restaurant business is a business of non-professionals; by this I mean that anyone can open a restaurant. You do not even have to have any prior knowledge (imagine that); this is not true of most other professions. Subsequently, many people have no idea of what they are in for when they open a new restaurant. I also find that most people are unwilling to ask for help – a recipe for disaster that helps the nation have a 50-60% failure rate for restaurants within their first three years.

If you are going to open and/or run a new restaurant, you had better have a lot of prior knowledge in the industry (or be willing to pay for someone else to provide the knowledge). I make the claim that the restaurant business requires skills in six separate and permanent areas of knowledge (domains). The first domain is the obvious; you must know about food, and there is a lot to know about food, including all there is to know about food safety. Passion about food is not required, but it sure helps to love what you are doing (why are you doing this anyway?). The second also seems obvious, and that is what I call customer relations or having good people skills. The hospitality industry requires taking care of people and their concerns, repeatedly, in an effective manner. You want the customer to feel a sense of comfort up to and beyond their expectations in order to produce in them a willingness to return (again and again), with service provided in such a way that they tell their friends and family about their experience. The third domain of knowledge is that of retail sales. This is a retail business where we have goods and services for sale, and, to complicate matters, the goods are perishable. Managers at Wal-Mart do not have this problem. Those sweaters are not going to go bad and start stinking up the storeroom.

This requires a fourth domain of knowledge: the handling and processing of perishable items. It is important to order just what you need and have practices for using everything before it can no longer be used effectively (i.e., it has to be thrown out or you will poison someone). The fifth domain of knowledge needed is in finance. Included in this domain is back-office accounting, year-end accounting, payroll, cash flow, capital improvements, and cash handling; this is not just about counting the money. It is a crucial area if you want to fully understand how business works and functions effectively in that business. The final area of necessary knowledge is in marketing. Every business owner should have this as one of their primary concerns. How do you get people through your doors consistently while continuously attracting new customers? Good question.

This claim of six separate domains of knowledge is by no means complete and could be added to (I do not believe that it can be subtracted from) based on individual operations. Some additions would fall under one of the six domains that I have put forth above, for example, employee relations. I would put this under customer relations because your employees are also your customers, and you need to know how to work with them consistently and effectively. You also need to know how to get rid of employees you do not want – and you will (most likely) have more than a few of them.

Six Domains of Knowledge

1. Food
2. Customer Relations
3. Retail Sales
4. Manufacturing
5. Finance
6. Marketing

Most of us cannot work effectively in all the six domains listed above, and we need help from others to fulfill on our offer of a quality dining experience. This help can be a partner, hired employees, or outside services. It is important to know what you can do well and when you need to hire other people to help you cover all the domains well. No one person can take care of all the concerns listed above effectively and still take care of the many concerns not related to work (i.e., marriage, friendships, play, family, etc.).

Restaurant Failure

The reasons for restaurant failure are many and varied, but I would guess that any failure is due to breakdowns or lack of skills in two or more of the above six domains. (Okay, so it is not really a guess). Below I list what could be considered the top four reasons for restaurant failure.

Four Reasons for Failure

1. Undercapitalization
2. Inconsistency
3. Ineffective management
4. No or ineffective marketing

Not enough money, or what is usually called **Undercapitalization**, is where failure occurs most often in this business. Fundamentally, it is not knowing the true cost of operation when starting up and not having enough cash reserve to continue through this start-up crunch. An important and somewhat invisible cost to new operators is tax liability, including sales tax liability and payroll tax liability. During the first three months of operation in a restaurant that is projected to do $1,000,000.00 in sales, this tax liability number can be close to $20,000.00. Generally, sales tax liability is paid monthly, but if this is overlooked, it can become a big problem quickly. Payroll taxes can add up quickly also. If you use a payroll company, these taxes would be paid by you weekly to the processor, and they take care of the liability when it comes due. If you do the payroll in-house, you must be aware of how fast that liability mounts up.

Inconsistency is another reason for failure. It is important to maintain consistent food quality along with consistent presentation and service. Nothing hurts more than inconsistency in your menu items and service. Whereas average food served in an excellent manner consistently can be a reason for success, excellent food poorly or inconsistently served can result in business failure.

Consistency in the physical space means both inside and outside as well as in your marketing messages.

Another reason for failure is **Ineffective Management** and staffing. In the six domains of knowledge listed above, this falls under 'customer relations' and points to a poverty in people skills. The vast majority of aspiring restaurateurs fill their management ranks with friends. This is not a bad practice, as long as they have management experience appropriate to the restaurant business and they are willing to disagree with you openly. Let us face it, you are not going to be right all the time, and you need to know that. So, you need to have people around whom you respect and who will point out your mistakes, be they verbal or behavioral.

The fourth reason for failure is having little or no experience in marketing. **Ineffective Marketing** can be very damaging to a new restaurant. It is critically important to get new people through your doors daily, and this can be accomplished with either a simple or complex marketing plan. The importance here is to think about marketing and have a plan with appropriate details. More important than having a plan is actually doing something about marketing, about getting the word out about your good offer.

You did not get into this business to fail (I am going out on a limb here). Now that you know of the six domains of knowledge for running a restaurant, as well as the four reasons listed for failure, you do not have to worry – you are an expert. Unfortunately, that is how many people think: just because they "have an understanding" about it, they think that they "know" it and can do it this is so untrue, and it is another reason for failure (not just in the restaurant industry). Just about everybody gets paid for what they can do, not for what they understand – which is not to be confused with knowing, since knowing implies embodied knowledge. For example, if you need a line cook and hire someone who knows all about food and cooking but has never worked a busy line, they will not be able to effectively work in that situation, and you will not be getting what you are paying for. Your line cook understands but does not have the knowledge to do the job well; this is a subtle but important distinction.

But what can you do? Invent or borrow (steal) practices and be consistent with them. I want to offer an example in the domain of finance, specifically – back-office record keeping/accounting, to give you an idea of how to take care in one domain of knowledge.

Back-office record keeping and accounting are two different things entirely. Many people get a little glassy-eyed and rightly so when they think about having to do the accounting for their business. Accounting is a set of practices for paying taxes. Why would you want to learn how to do that? Accounting is not about "running" the business effectively. Back-office record keeping is the set of practices that provide the numbers you need to run your business, numbers to which you can refer and to base your decisions. These are your business metrics; knowing them and working with them are vital for survival and profitability. These practices should also track and provide the information necessary for your accountant so they can perform their function in a cost effective and timely manner. An important distinction between accounting and back-office record keeping is that accounting "closes" the year and files everything in the event of an audit. Why else would you do this? Back-office record keeping keeps the previous year(s) finances easily accessible for reference, comparison, and decision making.

By providing clear and concise information on a monthly, quarterly, and yearly basis, your back-office practices should provide important numbers for you and information that makes your accountant's job easy. This is easily done if you are consistent with your daily, weekly, and monthly practices. When you are effective in your practices, this will also save you time and money (i.e., accountant's time, your time). Of course, your job is to make everyone's job easier. Get good at it, and you will reduce expenses.

Practices

I define the word practice in such a way that allows us to be effective with any business actions we engage. A practice is any action, or set of actions, that effectively and consistently takes care of a concern over a long period of time. To run your restaurant well, you must have practices in many areas. In finance, there must be practices for each day, month, quarter, and year. Practices are something that you invent, borrow from your own previous experiences, steal from other restaurants, or that you hire a knowledgeable person to invent for you.

What information about your business do you need on a daily, weekly, or monthly basis? What questions do you always seem to want answered quickly and easily? These questions, and questions like them, are your guide to inventing practices to take care of these concerns. Now you need the tools to get this information.

Tools

Tools are practices for either anticipating a problem or taking care of a problem in a specific domain of knowledge. When we call something a "tool," we are making a declaration about something being a practice. Normally, we consider only artifacts such as knives, telephones, and computers to be tools. We can, however, assess anything to be a tool, including people and businesses.

Tools are invented and "used" because they enable us to expand our possibilities for engaging in effective action. The desktop computer, for example, was invented to expand the space of possibilities for action beyond that of the adding machine or typewriter. It is not just important to have tools. We must also use them effectively or hire others to use them. A new slicer does a prep cook absolutely no good if they insist on cutting by hand. The point here is to acquire the necessary tools and use them in an effective manner to expand your possibilities and the possibilities of your restaurant (and increase your profits).

There are several tools available on the market to help in this domain. I am a fan of spreadsheet programs because of their simplicity and versatility. Of course, some people will not find them simple or versatile, but they really should accept the challenge of learning to use them.

Hire a Bookkeeper

If you can afford the $150 - $200 per week for a good bookkeeper, I recommend that you hire one. Ask around and find one who is neat, consistent, and reliable and who can work out of your office. Never forget, however, that you also must be able to do all or most of their job. Always know what is going on in your business! Make it a practice. In my experience, a good bookkeeper can take much better care of the books more consistently than you, as the owner or manager, can. How many times do you get interrupted when you are just trying to process payroll? They do not have your interruptions and can focus entirely on the job. Over a long period of time, they increase your time and energy to run your business (or take care of your family) for a very small expenditure.

Once you have effective practices in place for record keeping, it is important to have practices for referring to them. I know of a company that averages their past four week's income to estimate their next week's income. This may work for some businesses, but I do not believe that practice to be effective in the restaurant business. Businesses tend to have trends that show up on a yearly basis. Learn the trends of your business. By knowing these trends on a yearly basis, you are in a position to know when the slow and busy times will be and be prepared for them. Learn how to graph income (and/or meal counts) and expenses so you can see your trends on paper. The two largest expenses in this business are payroll and food. Just by knowing what to order and how to staff for each week will help save money and produce profit at the same time.

A Final Note

Like anything new, all this can seem overwhelming if you were to begin everything at the same time. There is a saying that is fitting here: 'If a boat could think of all the waves that would hit it on a transoceanic voyage, it would never leave the port.' Remember, all the waves will only come one at a time. Work in one domain of knowledge at a time. If you begin and learn one new practice, this is a great first step. If you are new to the business, start simply, take one thing that you can do now. Then add another one when you have mastered the previous one. It could be a two- or three-year project to get an efficient operation in place. Be patient with yourself while you make changes and learn new practices. What is important is your consistency with your own choice of practices and their effectiveness in taking care of you and your business in a timely way.

Running a successful business involves knowing what concerns you should be taking care of and consistently taking care of those concerns with effective practices. Here is the kicker; having effective practices takes practice (and time to learn them – just like learning anything for the first time). This will not happen overnight (although you might wish that it could). It takes a commitment to begin and a willingness to learn and practice – recurrently. Trust me. It will be worth the investment.

Of course, you do not have to do any of this. Just make it up on your own – which seems to work for some. After all, there are no right answers, and everything is always changing. Remember this: once you start to work effectively, and you take the time and do it well, you will never really be done. And, remember to have Fun!

Our Hidden Agenda

Note: This was written in 2019 for our 30th anniversary at The Vanilla Bean Café.

Since 1989, The Vanilla Bean Café, has operated in Pomfret, Connecticut, as a fast-casual restaurant and has been featured on television, magazines, newspapers, a cookbook, and online in various ways. However, the 'Bean' is more than what it appears to be. We have been keeping a secret. To our regular customer who visits us for a meal, it may seem like our core business model is providing quality hand-prepared food in a friendly limited-service environment. While this is true, we cannot fulfill on our offer if we do not have present, engaged, and committed employees. Our primary concern as operators has expanded from our commitment to proper food handling and overall consistent quality to creating an environment that attracts the right employee and then educating and training these people to be great at what they do. Essentially, our employees are our most valuable asset. The ones who are working with us today help to ensure that there is a job with us in the future for other employees, thereby helping us to be a sustainable business and job creator.

We work to create a restaurant that entices the 'right' person to want to work here or to 'self-select' and apply for a job with us. We have not advertised for employees in the traditional way in over 25 years. We always hire based on current employee recommendations, as well as our customer recommendations. We also are firm believers in nepotism, as we have had great success with that since our beginnings, including ourselves. We are, after all, a family business.

It is not just about creating the environment where the right employee 'shows up.' It is also about creating meaningful and fun work with teams that like to work together, be challenged, engaged, and appreciated. We have developed several work philosophies that help us with our mission of creating a space in which a young person can learn and thrive. We are essentially an entry-level job that comes with lots of education and training to help them become a great employee, not just in the moment, but as an embodied practice that will help them to succeed in whatever future employment awaits them or whatever entrepreneurial adventure they take. We, along with most other restaurants, help to educate and train the future workforce. Half of all adults have worked in the restaurant industry at some point during their lives. In fact, nearly one in three Americans had their first job at a restaurant. It is because of this that we take seriously the development of our young employees. What they learn with us can have a great effect on them throughout their careers. While we know that most of them will not stay with us for more than three to four years, we get a great co-worker in the moment and know that we have helped a young person get a good start in their future work endeavors. It is important to note here that we do this for ourselves as well as for the employees. Our management is Selfishly Altruistic.

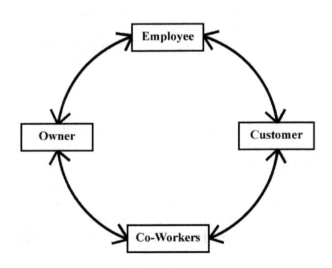

One of our main philosophies is asking our employees the question, 'Who Do You Work For?' It is essential that they understand the reason they are here is for themselves and the future they are working to create. Sure, they have short-term goals of gaining work experience, making money and friends, etc. While the owners make the work possible and specifies the rules within which the work is performed (the rules are also specified by the federal and state governments), it is the employee who works for themselves, to be the best they can be in the moment, to embody effective working practices that will become their foundation for all jobs they encounter in their future. In our philosophy, the employee works for (in this order): Themselves, The Customer, Their Co-Workers, and then The Owners (or people who make it possible). This is all set up in what is called an action workflow circle (see graphic) that has the employer working for the employee and their co-workers to take care of the customer to effectively fulfill on our offer. If the employee is not here for themselves with some story about their future, we find that they may not be a good fit for our workplace. We can help them too if they are willing to make changes in their life and accept responsibility for their future, but they must make that choice.

We empower the employees to create their own teams. They can specify with whom they want to work and, more importantly, with whom they do not want to work. We are firm believers in not tolerating slackers and whiners as employees and encourage our teams to not put up with co-workers who are obviously not working with and for the team. We do not fire people often, but when we do, it is because they do not embody the practice of working for each other. Employees can recommend their co-workers for further education or termination (or, as we like to say, they get to 'vote people off the island'). We also get to teach people how to quit if the job is not what they had in mind or what they want to do. It may sound weird, but people are not taught how to quit in an effective manner that actually helps them and the future they are working to create.

Because of the effort we put into being a place where people want to work, we tend to keep employees longer than the industry average, especially in our primary age group of 17- to 23-year-olds. Many employees love to work here and stay with us from high school and summers throughout their college years. We pay them a little better than comparable jobs and really work to create a space in which they get to have Fun, as well as learn things. We are always cross training staff and teaching them whatever they step up to learn. We keep in touch with many of our former employees and are happy to see them succeed, many in the restaurant business. There are four restaurants in this area owned by former employees.

So here we are celebrating 30 years of business, and we are also celebrating 30 years of all the employees who have worked with us during that time. We could not have done it without them, and our hope is that their world of work is just that much better for having worked and learned effective practices with us. So, when you patronize our establishment(s), you are not only getting what you came in for. Please know that you are helping young people create a more effective future for themselves and others. We thank you.

Tai Chi and the Practice of Business

Tai Chi is an internal Chinese martial art that many people practice for health and wellness. It is a soft style of martial art that requires the muscles' complete relaxation to the greatest possible extent. Many practitioners use Tai Chi as a form of meditation in motion. Tai Chi has gained in popularity over the last 20 years, and its reputation for alleviating the effects of aging has become more well-known. Communities around the world (hospitals, clinics, community centers, and senior centers) are all hosting Tai Chi classes. As a result of this popularity, there are many reasons that people practice Tai Chi. Some practice Tai Chi primarily for deepening their martial arts in fighting, others for its aesthetic appeal, while many practice for achieving personal benefits, mental and physical.

Researchers have found that long-term Tai Chi practice has had favorable effects on the promotion of balance control, flexibility, and cardiovascular fitness. Other studies have shown that it reduces pain, stress, and anxiety in healthy subjects. While all this is well-substantiated and the health benefits of Tai Chi have been well documented, there has been little written about using the basic principles of Tai Chi in the practice of running an effective business.

There are three elements of Tai Chi that I have incorporated into my life and my business. These elements are Ground, Center, and Balance. Ground is the story from which I act. Center is the place from which I act. Balance is that which I work to achieve and maintain through my actions.

The 'Ground' from which we practice Tai Chi is the story that gives the movements and postures meaning and purpose. The Ground represents the martial application of each movement along with the health and wellness it promotes. My Ground for acting in business is the tradition or story of business itself, an existing story that I couple with my own reasons for doing what I do to produce purpose and meaning. My Ground is essentially the story I tell, a story that becomes the offer that I create and allows for the growth of a business from which other people may benefit. I too benefit, since I earn an income that I use to take care of the other concerns I have simply by being human (i.e., shelter, food, clothing, etc.).

'Center' in Tai Chi is the powerful place from which we move and act. It is referred to as the *dantian* (dan t'ian, dan tien or tan t'ien). It is described as an important focus point for internal meditation and refers specifically to the physical center of gravity located in the abdomen. If a person is not centered, their form loses power and effectiveness, and the practitioner becomes unbalanced and compromised. My Center in the practice of business is produced by My Ground or story that includes my reasons for all that I am doing. I avoid wasting time, energy, or resources on issues or situations that are not a part of what I am working to achieve. I avoid what I call 'time bandits,' people who waste my time on meaningless situations and keep me from working in a timely and effective manner on what I do care about. Staying centered or mindful of My Purpose helps me to avoid or spend less time with these 'time bandits.' Staying centered is also important when dealing with employees and customers. I work to understand what they want and/or need as I perform to fulfill their needs while staying true to myself and my business. I also find that moving from the *dantian* in my daily routines helps to keep me focused and balanced, even when conditions become stressful.

'Balance' in Tai Chi is the somatic balance or the balance of the physical body. It is also the balance of yin and yang, the balance of softness and stickiness with hardness and force. In the practice of business, it is very much the same. Using force in business may yield short-term gains but comes with long-term consequences. Moving softly – building long-term relationships that work well for many – can be much more effective. Questions I often ask include: 'Am I fulfilling my offers without doing more or less than I need to satisfy the customer(s)?'; 'Do I work effectively in stressful situations, without over or under exerting?'; 'Do I tense up and react without being mindful?' And most important: 'Am I appropriately taking time away from business to keep my whole life balanced?' For example, 'Do I spend time with family and friends and take time to exercise?'

Tai Chi's martial aspect relies on sensitivity to the opponent's movements and center of gravity for dictating appropriate responses. In the practice of business, I pay attention to current trends and my rivals to see where the marketplace is moving, and I engage in appropriate responses to meet those changing conditions. I attempt to avoid tensing up or reacting to every little change in the marketplace or to every situation I encounter daily. I am relaxed, and I move in a grounded, centered, and balanced way to take care of myself, my business, and my future. In so doing, I also help to take care of my health and well-being. As I continue to practice Tai Chi and the principles thereof, I find that I take better care of whatever it is that I am presently doing whenever I am mindful enough. The longer I practice Tai Chi, the better I get at incorporating its elements into my life and my business.

Managing Mood

While you are practicing changing your own narrative and improving your own practice, here are a few things you can work on as well.

Distance yourself from your mood. Moods are fleeting emotions; they are not the core of your being. Repeat a statement like this: "This mood isn't who I am and is only something I'm experiencing." Then focus on what outcome you want in the given situation that will be effective for all concerned.

Do something. Moods, no matter what they are, have a way of paralyzing us. Acknowledge your mood and then act in a way that does not create negative consequences and fits with your narrative. You do not have to wait until you feel better to act.

Practice mindfulness. Instead of fixating on your mood, use your senses – seeing, hearing, smelling, etc. – to pull yourself out of your head, out of your funk, and into the present moment. Then, find something that is positive on which to focus.

Pause and breathe. When you feel a negative mood begin to take hold, take a moment to pause, breathe deeply, and focus. Center your attention on what is immediate in the moment, such as the sound of your breathing or the feeling of the temperature on your skin. By focusing your attention on something sensory, you can take your mind away from negative thoughts and feelings. If you feel overpowered during a bad mood and tend to lose rationality, sit down afterward and really think about what happened. Examine the event that changed your mood in relation to your reaction and come up with a positive way of reacting to the same situation in the future.

Improve your lifestyle. Assess your lifestyle and attempt to restore balance in all areas of your life. Ensure that you get enough exercise, sleep, and eat a balanced diet. Address unhealthy habits like excessive drinking or high sugar intake. Find productive ways to deal with stress, anger, and anxiety. Sometimes the solution to moodiness is as simple as changing diet, exercise, or sleep patterns. Other times, moodiness may suggest a more serious problem. That is when you may need to ask for professional help.

With mindful practice in observing your moods, coupled with a long-term story of care, you can work to change your mood in any situation and, in so doing, change the mood of the environment you are in. Once you are adept in managing your own mood, you will be able to begin work on managing the mood of the entire workplace. In business and in leadership, this is crucial for taking care of your team and the long-term viability of yourself and the business.

This all takes time and practice; it will not be accomplished overnight. Like learning anything new, you must be patient and forgiving with yourself while you are on this path.

The Final Stitch

"The path to your dreams is rarely linear. You gotta zig-zag your way to happiness." - Karen Salmansohn

This is the real Last Page, the other one was the penultimate page, but it would have looked ridiculous if I had called it that. You have wandered through all the preceding pages and meandered through the many sections of the Appendix, and now, here you are. Congratulations! I too, love to finish a book. But you are not done. I think you already know that. Challenges await.

What you have is this moment of Now, a story about your life that mobilizes you into action and a promise of a bright path that leads into an unknown future (albeit a zig-zagging path). My hope is that you have learned practices that will open more possibilities for you on that path and that you have learned to embody these practices in a way that will allow you to experience and accept new challenges.

To make the most of this book, it is good to re-read chapters that were meaningful to you. It is great to share this book with other like-minded people in your life. Quilters will often get together to share knowledge to expand and hone their own talents (this is true of most artisans and professionals). We learn best when we share the learning with others and spend time together discussing ideas and practices that we find helpful and meaningful.

In quilting, when you take on the challenging stitch and complete The Drunkard's Path, you are well on your way to a new and beautiful quilt and the possibilities of even more intricate designs. In your own life, when you learn something new and take on a difficult challenge, you open your own future to a space of beautiful new possibilities.

And always, Have Fun, Learn Things!

I don't claim to have all the answers
And I've got my share of questions
But if I don't follow blindly
It doesn't mean I've lost my way
I'm still on the journey
Headed down the road less traveled
I guess we're all gonna get there
In our own time and way

- Copyright © Bill Miller, 2000 *The Vision*

Further Reading List

Books on Philosophy

The Four Agreements – A Toltec Wisdom Book – by don Miguel Ruiz
The Tao of Leadership: Lao Tzu's Tao Te Ching Adapted for a New Age – by John Heider
Change Your Thoughts, Change Your Life: Living the Wisdom of the Tao – by Dr. Wayne W. Dyer
Your Erroneous Zones – by Dr. Wayne W. Dyer
Man's Search For Meaning - by Viktor E. Frankl
A Brief History of Everything – by Ken Wilber
The Biology Of Belief: Unleashing The Power Of Consciousness, Matter And Miracles – by Bruce H. Lipton
The Tree of Knowledge: The Biological Roots of Human Understanding – by Humberto R. Maturana and Francisco J. Varela
E-Squared: Nine Do-It-Yourself Energy Experiments That Prove Your Thoughts Create Your Reality – by Pam Grout
Understanding Computers and Cognition: A New Foundation for Design – by Terry Winograd and Fernando Flores
Meditations – by Marcus Aurelius
Tao: The Watercourse Way – by Alan Watts
Buddhism Plain and Simple – by Steve Hagen

Books on Leadership

Leadership Is an Art – by Max DePree
The 7 Habits of Highly Effective People: Powerful Lessons in Personal Change – by Stephen R. Covey
Start with Why: How Great Leaders Inspire Everyone to Take Action – by Simon Sinek
Emotional Intelligence – by Daniel Goleman Ph.D.
Trust Factor: The Science of Creating High-Performance Companies – Paul J. Zak
No Excuses!: The Power of Self-Discipline – by Brian Tracy

Leadership and the New Science: Discovering Order in a Chaotic World – by Margaret J. Wheatley
Setting the Table: The Transforming Power of Hospitality in Business – by Danny Meyer
The Virgin Way: If It's Not Fun, It's Not Worth Doing – by Richard Branson
Dare to Lead: Brave Work. Tough Conversations. Whole Hearts – by Brené Brown Ph.D.

Audio Books

The Power of Vulnerability: Teachings of Authenticity, Connection, and Courage – by Brené Brown Ph.D.
Out of Your Mind – by Alan Watts

Interesting Books on Food

Salt, Fat, Acid, Heat: Mastering the Elements of Good Cooking – Samin Nosrat
Appetites: A Cookbook Hardcover – by Anthony Bourdain
Unmentionable Cuisine – by Calvin W. Schwabe
The Flavor Bible: The Essential Guide to Culinary Creativity, Based on the Wisdom of America's Most Imaginative Chefs – by Karen Page

Works Cited

Beckwith, LaSharnda, Dr. *It's Your Life; Own It!: No Blame, No Excuses.* AuthorHouse Publishing Company, 2014.

Bits & Pieces. Ragan Communications, www.ragan.com, 1994-2020

Branson, Richard. *The Virgin Way: If It's Not Fun, It's Not Worth Doing.* Portfolio, Penguin Random House, 2015.

Bridges, Frances. *"How To Stop Taking Things Personally." Forbes*, Forbes Magazine, 29 June 2018, www.forbes.com/sites/francesbridges/2018/06/29/how-to-stop-taking-things-personally/?sh=2f17d3726726. Accessed November 2019.

Brown, Brené, Ph.D. *The Power of Vulnerability: Teachings of Authenticity, Connection, and Courage.* Sounds True, 2013. Audio Book.

Carricarte, Lindsay. *"It's Not About You: 7 Tips & Quotes to Stop Taking It Personally."* Elephant Journal, Waylon H. Lewis Enterprises, 18 May 2017, www.elephantjournal.com/2017/05/its-not-about-you-7-tips-quotes-to-stop-taking-it-personally. Accessed January 2020.

Dawkins, Richard. *The Selfish Gene.* 2nd Ed., Oxford University Press, 1989.

DePree, Max. *Leadership Is an Art.* Currency, 2011.

Dyer, Dr. Wayne W. *Change Your Thoughts, Change Your Life: Living the Wisdom of the Tao.* Hay House, Inc., 2007.

Flores, Fernando. *Conversations for Action and Collected Essays: Instilling a Culture of Commitment in Working.* Createspace, 2013.

Frankl, Viktor E. *Man's Search For Meaning.* Beacon Press, 1992.

Heider, John. *The Tao of Leadership: Lao Tzu's Tao Te Ching Adapted for a New Age.* Humanics Publishing Group, 1985.

Maturana, Humberto R., and Francisco J. Varela. *The Tree of Knowledge: The Biological Roots of Human Understanding.* Shambhala Publications, 1992.

McCammon, Ross. *Works Well with Others: An Outsider's Guide to Shaking Hands, Shutting up, Handling Jerks, and Other Crucial Skills in Business That No One Ever Teaches You.* Penguin, 2016.

Nosrat, Samin. *Salt, Fat, Acid, Heat: Mastering the Elements of Good Cooking.* Simon and Schuster, 2017.

Ruiz, Miguel. *The Four Agreements - A Toltec Wisdom Book.* Amber-Allen Publishing, Inc., 2008.

Schwabe, Calvin W. *Unmentionable Cuisine.* University of Virginia Press, 1996.

Tracy, Brian. *No Excuses!: The Power of Self-Discipline.* Vanguard Press, 2011.

Winograd, Terry, and Fernando Flores. *Understanding Computers and Cognition: A New Foundation for Design.* Addison Wesley Publishing Co., 1987.

Zak, Paul J. *Trust Factor: The Science of Creating High-Performance Companies.* AMACOM Div American Mgmt Assn, 2017.

A note about the quotes used in this book – I have been collecting quotes that resonate with me since 1994 and have been publishing them in our quarterly newsletter, *Bean Soup*, since that time. Many of the quotes in this book have been culled from my collection.

Images used in this book

Figure 1 – Perspective – No copyright information available.

Figure 2 – Dawn & Dusk quilt by D. Hervieux 1996 – owned by Barry Jessurun.

Figure 3 – The Yes Path – part of The Basic Conversation for Action from the book *Understanding Computers and Cognition: A New Foundation for Design* – by Terry Winograd and Fernando Flores. Addison-Wesley Publishing Company 1987 – used with permission.

Figure 4 – Who Do You Work For? – Copyright Barry Jessurun.

Figure 5 – The Yes Path – part of The Basic Conversation for Action from the book *Understanding Computers and Cognition: A New Foundation for Design* – by Terry Winograd and Fernando Flores. Addison-Wesley Publishing Company 1987 – used with permission.

Figure 6 – The Basic Conversation for Action from the book *Understanding Computers and Cognition: A New Foundation for Design* – by Terry Winograd and Fernando Flores. Addison-Wesley Publishing Company 1987 – used with permission.

Figure 7 – Who Do You Work For? – Copyright Barry Jessurun.

Figure 8 – The Basic Conversation for Action from the book *Understanding Computers and Cognition: A New Foundation for Design* – by Terry Winograd and Fernando Flores. Addison-Wesley Publishing Company 1987 – used with permission.

Figure 9 – Balance Diagram – Copyright Barry Jessurun.

Figure 10 – Drunkard's Path Heart Stitch – No copyright information available.

Gratitude

Sticking with the book's theme, I am sure you know that I did not do create and publish a book all by myself. I had help from many people along the way. Like a soup that becomes better with input from many knowledgeable people, this book is a better version of itself from the help and input of many of my friends, co-workers, and colleagues.

First, I want to thank all my staff, past and present, even the troublemakers, you know who you are. I have worked with over 2,000 people and have learned valuable lessons and ideas from many of them. It is because of them that I even have a book to write.

The Business Professionals Course, now Ajinet, the education program I began in 1997 and continued until 2002. I learned many things from this course and was exposed to new thinking. Most importantly, my main teacher, Toby Hecht, encouraged us to write to explore to understand concepts more effectively. So, I did.

I wish to thank Paul McNamara for introducing me to this course. It was the foundation I needed to expand my knowledge and grow my business.

I am grateful for many of my classmates from that course, but mostly to my friend Mike Stefaniak, with whom I had numerous conversations that helped to deepen our learning and understanding.

I would not have accomplished much of what I have done without one key employee who has been with me for many years. Kayla Densmore has been with me for over 20 years in many key roles. She was also a reader of the second draft and offered constructive feedback that helped shape and strengthen the narrative.

Over the years, Sarah Matteau, our current general manager at The Vanilla Bean Café, has read almost everything I have written for the business. She was a second draft reader and offered advice from simple edits to the better crafting of sentences to convey the proper meaning.

Christine Kalafus took the time to help me understand the publishing business and shared with me what I needed to do to become a published author.

William Moylan Jr., a visiting professor at Eastern Connecticut State University who continually invites me to his business and entrepreneur classes to speak with his students. It is through those talks that I was able to imagine the structure of this book.

I wish to thank my first-round editor, Brad Davis, whose edits, comments, and suggestions helped strengthen the first draft and made it a cohesive manuscript.

I am profoundly grateful for Donna Ayres-LaPointe, my bookkeeper since 1999 and a second draft editor who helped with minor edits, grammatical formatting and offered constructive feedback on the text.

Elizabeth (Zim) Zimmerman was helpful with her edits and feedback on the concept paper for The Drunkard's Path title and also helped in crafting the back cover text. It is not easy to take four paragraphs and shorten them to something short, meaningful, and to the point. Her input on the front and back cover design helped tremendously.

Megan Feragne, a long-time employee and family friend, a second draft reader who offered feedback and edits that no one else saw. She and I also engaged in many meaningful discussions that helped shape some of the content in the book.

Emily Cole, a long-time employee at Dog Lane Café and English Major at UCONN, a second draft reader who was very thorough in her edits and offered helpful and encouraging comments.

Monique Sourinho, for the creating the cover photo and for engaging and meaningful conversations that helped in the development of this book.

Natalie Susi, my long-distance entrepreneur friend and one of my second daft readers who offered tremendous feedback on all aspects of the book. Her suggestions from chapter titles to book structure were instrumental for the final draft of this book—much gratitude.

Melissa Brown, a longtime employee, and friend for many years, she was a second draft reader who went through the text twice to offer simple edits and meaningful changes within chapters to create a stronger narrative and other miscellaneous help.

The final proofread was done by Jamie Shaw, whom I contacted at the last minute, and she came through quickly and with flying colors. The clean version of this book is due to your years of experience and sharp eye.

Katie Walsh, you showed up when I needed you. What started as a final round editing job turned into final draft editing and book formatting. Katie also offered the help I needed to get the book to the finish line. Her support and insight as an editor made the final draft, and the book come to fruition.

Much love and gratitude to Maria Sangiolo, my wife and life partner. Thank you for all your help and love along the way, including edits, comments, and the encouragement to keep the project going to the end. I love you to the moon and back. Together we are more.

© Nonni Muller 2021 - www.nonniphotography.com

About Barry Jessurun

Barry is the President of Green Valley Hospitality, a restaurant group that oversees four restaurant concepts in Northeastern Connecticut. He lives in the Quiet Corner of Connecticut with his wife, Maria Sangiolo; together, they have raised two children. Barry has been managing and working with young people his whole career. He approaches business with a passion, a keen sense of quality, and an innate sense of hospitality. He is an avid squash player, and he has been practicing Tai Chi since 1999. He incorporates its eastern philosophy into the operation of his businesses, his relationships, and his writing.

CPSIA information can be obtained
at www.ICGtesting.com
Printed in the USA
BVHW091226290621
610728BV00006B/1914